LABOR IN ACTION
The Story of the American Labor Movement

The labor strikes and disturbances which beset our nation today are not new. Since 1636 when a group of Maine fishermen were refused their pay, capital and labor have been in constant dispute. Every era in our history has been marked by attempts at unionization and improved labor-management relations. In this book the author discusses the labor movement and traces its growth to the present day. LABOR IN ACTION will give readers a better understanding of today's labor-management problems and a basis for judging the issues for themselves.

Books by Adrian A. Paradis

BUSINESS IN ACTION

LABOR IN ACTION
The Story of the American Labor Movement

GOVERNMENT IN ACTION
How Our Federal Government Works

LABOR IN ACTION

The Story of the American Labor Movement

by ADRIAN A. PARADIS

Julian Messner   New York

Published by Julian Messner
Division of Pocket Books, Inc.
8 West 40th Street, New York 10018

© Copyright 1963 by Adrian A. Paradis

Fourth Printing, 1966

We wish to thank the following for the use of their pictures: American
Federation of Labor and Congress of Industrial Organizations, Association
of American Railroads, Eugene V. Debs Foundation, George Eastman
House, Hughes Aircraft Company, International Ladies' Garment Workers'
Union, Rockefeller Center, Inc., United Automobile Workers, United Mine
Workers.

Printed in the United States of America
Library of Congress Catalog Card No.: 63-16798

Contents

5

Contents

1 ⊂⊐

The Beginnings

THE TINY WOODEN SAILING VESSEL TWISTED AND TURNED as it bobbed up and down in the North Atlantic gale. Terrifying wave after wave slapped it and tossed it about until it seemed the boat would surely sink. Crowded into its hold were some three hundred men and women who were making their way to America. Some were praying that the ship would not sink, many were too sick to care, a few had already died of scurvy, disease or malnutrition. By the time the boat docked at Philadelphia in the spring of 1653 only half of the passengers were still alive.

"Everyone on shore!" the captain ordered as soon as the boat had tied up to the wharf. Scarcely able to walk after the long and terrible voyage, the half-starved passengers staggered across the gangplank to firm ground. Those who had signed articles of indenture before they left England were met at the dock by their masters, who had arranged to pay their fare upon arrival in the colonies. Anyone who could not find immediate employment was sold by the ship's captain to colonists anxious to obtain laborers.

The terms of servitude under which white men and women agreed to work varied from one to seven years, the usual period being four. In the southern colonies where labor was supplied by the African slave trade, servitude was usually permanent, and, of course, this applied to all Negro children born thereafter.

NEED FOR WORKERS

The founders of each colony quickly discovered that they needed additional settlers. Forests had to be cleared, roads built, houses, churches and public buildings erected, crops grown, shoes and clothing made. Many of these tasks required skilled workers, but because of the lack of artisans the early colonists had to learn the trades of shoemaker, weaver, mason and carpenter.

Governor John Winthrop noted that many skilled laborers had left the Massachusetts colony to work for higher wages in newer frontier towns or had turned to farming. By 1630 the shortage became so acute that the General Court established a wage ceiling of two shillings a day for bricklayers, carpenters, sawyers, joiners, thatchers and other skilled artisans and eighteen pence for all laborers. Workers were forbidden to change occupations, and various distinctions in dress were decreed to keep the laboring classes in their place.

While the new colonies were experiencing labor problems, many Englishmen were asserting that Great Britain was suffering from overpopulation. As a solution they suggested sending people to the colonies. The idea caught hold, and in 1619 some four hundred children were rounded up from the slums, given to the Virginia Company and sent to America to be sold as indentured servants. Soon misleading and often fraudulent advertisements appeared throughout England urging men and women to sign up as indentured servants and go to America, a land where every man had opportunity to own land and where food was so plentiful it practically dropped into one's mouth. The colonial market for laborers became so great that ship captains were kidnapping young English boys and adults and selling them in America.

Although most of the laborers sold as servants were unskilled, this was not entirely the case. An advertisement that appeared in the *Virginia Gazette* of March 28, 1771, indicated the variety of occupations found among the men on this one ship:

Just arrived at Leedstown, the Ship Justitia, with about One Hundred Healthy Servants.

Men, Women and Boys, among which are many Tradespeople—viz. Blacksmiths, Shoemakers, Tailors, House Carpenters and Joiners, a Cooper, several Silversmiths, Weavers, A Jeweler, and many others. The Sale will commence on Tuesday, the 2nd. of April, at Leedstown on Rappahannock River. A reasonable Credit will be allowed, giving Bond with Approved Security to

Thomas Hodge

Overlooking no possible source of settlers, the British authorities decided to ship out all felons in order to save the expense of maintaining so many prisons. Now the boats were hauling convicted criminals across the Atlantic, royal pardon having been granted to those who permitted themselves to be sold as servants. To the great consternation of many Americans, load upon load of convicts, paupers and political prisoners arrived in America, about 50,000 altogether, most of them going to the southern colonies.

"We apparently lose our reputation, while we are believed to be a place only fit to receive such base and lewd persons," complained a member of the Council of the General Court of Virginia. Protesting in stronger language, Benjamin Franklin wrote in 1769 to the *London Chronicle*: "Their emptying their jails into our settlements is an insult and a contempt, the cruelest that ever one people offered to another."

The importation of white indentured servants, both skilled and unskilled, did not solve the labor problem. Once most of these immigrants had served their terms they moved west, where they obtained cheap land and became yeomen farmers. The South augmented its labor force by continuing to import Negro slaves, few of whom ever won their freedom. Although large numbers of Europeans came to the other colonies, a labor shortage persisted until the early part of the nineteenth century.

ROLE OF THE CRAFTSMEN

Most of the first settlers not only raised their own food but also had to make much of their own clothing, furniture, tools and utensils. In a short time, however, the services of skilled craftsmen became more and more in demand as towns grew and frontiers gradually pushed westward. Many of the artisans traveled about the country from farm to farm working wherever needed and often plying several different trades. These men were called journeymen. As villages turned into towns and towns became cities, the itinerant journeymen could not meet all the demands for specialized services, and the more ambitious craftsmen set up their own bakery, printing, shoemaking, tailoring, hat or cabinet shops. In such establishments

10

a master workman employed journeymen laborers who might include one or two skilled mechanics and artisans. In addition there might be a boy serving as an apprentice.

Orders that came into a shop were called "bespoke work." The men and boys often worked in the master's home and even boarded with him, working side by side in a leisurely, relaxed atmosphere. Workers enjoyed good security, for labor was scarce and usually there were laws that restrained dismissal and provided for apprenticeships.

Gradually, aggressive individuals established various little mills and factories throughout the colonies and employed both skilled and unskilled labor. These tiny industries made a wide variety of articles ranging from paper, rope, gunpowder and cotton cloth to iron products, pewter, glass, brick, tools and hardware. Such products were sold locally or shipped abroad as trade between the colonies and England increased.

Many workmen did not enjoy political liberty. In numerous cities and towns only property owners were permitted to vote. In spite of their importance to society, artisans, mechanics and unskilled laborers had little or no voice in their government or in legislation that affected them directly. The Declaration of Independence, which said that all men were created equal, did little to help, and even Thomas Jefferson was opposed to giving labor a vote, fearing that such men, not being landowners, might not be a good influence for a republican form of government.

Although they could not vote, many workers were vitally interested in the affairs of their colony. The various patriotic societies that pushed first for justice from England and then for independence consisted mostly of laborers, artisans and mechanics. They objected to oppression from England as well as from those who ruled in the colonies. This inclination to speak out and if necessary fight for what they felt was right would someday encourage them to seek better working conditions for the laboring man. Prior to 1800, however, the economy of the thirteen colonies was primarily based on agriculture and small handicraft industries. There was little strife between masters and employees, but from time to time there were signs of coming labor troubles in the new country.

EARLY LABOR PROBLEMS

A thick fog surrounded Richmond Island, which stands just off the coast of Maine below Portland. A boat appeared gradually through the mist and drew up to the rocky shore. A rope reached out, caught around a tree, and soon the long vessel eased to the shore.

The men spotted their boss, Robert Trelauney, a tall man who was watching from the cliff below.

"We've had a good catch!" one of the fishermen shouted as he pointed to the mound of fish in the big boat. "Earned our wages all right this time," he added.

"I'm not paying you now," Mr. Trelauney declared. "You'll have to wait for your money."

Whereupon, according to reports, the men fell "into a mutiny"—this, in 1636, being the first recorded labor disturbance in America.

Some forty years later the licensed cartmen of New York assembled near the Battery.

"From now on you men will take the dirt from the street for three pence a load," the boss informed them. The cartmen not only protested the low wages but also "combined to refuse full compliance."

In 1768 journeymen tailors in New York held a "turnout,"

12

or strike, because their wages were reduced. They even inserted an advertisement in the newspaper defying their masters and offering to take private work. This may have been the first genuine strike of employees against their employers, and it was soon followed by other "turnouts" as spiraling living costs were not matched with pay increases.

Journeymen throughout the colonies were learning that the only way to force their masters to recognize their demands for higher pay was to agree among themselves on what they wanted and then "turn out" if necessary. "Turning out" generally meant staying at home until the dispute was settled. There were few disturbances, but the workers of that day were aware of the need to stick together.

Although workers were gradually beginning to adopt the turnout to enforce demands for fairer wages, it was not until the end of the eighteenth century that they formed associations for this purpose. Long before the Revolutionary War many masters and journeymen had joined trade societies which had been formed to provide for their members sick and death benefits, social activities and the use of club or meeting rooms. In Boston, New York and Philadelphia, by the time George Washington was inaugurated men engaged in practically every trade had organized such societies. Some of these were linked together loosely by regional organizations such as the Association of Mechanics of the Commonwealth of Massachusetts, the Albany Mechanics Society, and the General Society of Merchants and Tradesmen in New York.

The early workmen's societies were not concerned with economic activities, hours of labor, wages or working conditions. In fact, the New York Society of Journeymen Shipwrights had a provision in its charter that stated the organization must be dissolved if ever an attempt were made to fix wages.

THE FIRST UNIONS

A group of shoemaker journeymen in Philadelphia organized a society in 1792. However, it lasted only a year before the men abandoned it. It was not long before they recognized the need for some association through which they could band together if they hoped to better their working conditions, and in 1794 they successfully reorganized the group. That same year the Typographical Society was founded by New York printers, and in Philadelphia a delegation of cordwainers (shoemakers) met with the master shoemakers and worked out an agreement. Other groups of skilled workers organized associations or trade societies. These were not unions as we know them today but local associations restricted to one craft. The usual initiation fee for new association members was fifty cents, and monthly dues varied between six and ten cents.

Many of these groups also sought to enforce a closed shop by compelling their masters to hire only association men. Members of an association might agree on a wage scale and promise that they would not work for an employer who would not pay that rate. Woe to any new journeyman who came to town and refused to join the association. Not only was it difficult for such a man to find a job but he was socially ostracized. No association member would live in the same house with him, let alone eat at the same table! The most serious problem to skilled labor was the runaway apprentice who would work for less money than an association man.

These first labor organizations were watched carefully by the masters, many of whom resented having their journeymen dictate what wages should be paid as well as the terms of working conditions. Some masters did not hesitate to go to court to stop this threat to their independence.

"Conspiracy is what this is!" they told the judges. "These men who work for us are in a conspiracy against us."

Several cases were brought by the masters against the shoemaker unions. In the first, which was heard in Philadelphia, the jury found six men guilty of going out on strike for higher wages. Three years later twenty-four New Yorkers were fined for a criminal conspiracy involving a strike, and in 1815 an association of shoemakers was indicted in Pittsburgh on similar grounds.

At the beginning of the nineteenth century prospects of the craftsmen obtaining justice from the courts looked black indeed. It was even worse for the masses of unskilled laborers who had no associations or societies to represent them and were completely at the mercy of their employers. Unless the courts changed their interpretation of the law or labor was allowed to assert itself, the situation was likely to remain the same.

THE BIG CHANGE

The prosperous-looking merchant strode into the small shop where the master and his four journeymen were making shoes. It was 1810 and business was good.

"I'm ordering shoes," he announced. "Are you interested in supplying me with two dozen pairs?"

The master rose from his bench and squinted at the tall stranger. No one had ever given him such a large order. Most of the "bespoke" orders were for one or two pairs.

"What are you going to do with all those shoes?" he asked suspiciously. "You can't sell them here in town."

"Of course not, but I can market them in New York or Philadelphia or other large cities. Once I was a master shoemaker myself," he continued, "then I made money buying and selling land. Now I'm a merchant. Don't make shoes any more —I sell 'em. Now tell me, how much do you want for a pair?"

The master named his price and the merchant doubled over with laughter.

"That's ridiculous," he said. "I can get them much cheaper from the old country. You'll all starve to death if you keep charging those prices."

How was the master to know that all America was changing and that his little business was already caught in this shift? The days of the craftsman were numbered as the merchant capitalist grew in importance. With more and more people pushing out into the western frontiers and with the appearance first of better roads and later the canals and railroads, it now became possible to ship goods over great distances to new markets.

Initially the merchant capitalist imported goods from Europe at cheap prices because labor there was poorly paid; then he found it even more profitable to organize factories in the United States and do his own manufacturing here. Now the craftsman was really in trouble. Many of the handmade products which he fashioned with such care and pride could not compete with similar mass-produced items. He could not afford to have his wages reduced, but if he made any organized efforts to protest, he risked trouble with the courts. As for his unskilled brothers—they could anticipate an even worse fate, as they would soon become industrial slaves working in mines, mills, factories, and for railroads or large and small businesses.

Little wonder that in the early nineteenth century many people asked themselves if the American workingman who had won the War of Independence had lost his personal liberty.

2

The Struggle for Recognition

THE LOWELL GIRLS

THE LINE OF GIRLS WAITING TO MARCH EXTENDED TWO MILES up the road leading into Lowell, Massachusetts. It was June 27, 1833, and just before noon, when ceremonies were to start, the sun burst through the clouds that had hung over the city for several days. At a signal from the marshal the first pair of young women started toward the Merrimack House, where President Andrew Jackson was waiting to review the unusual procession.

"Very pretty women, by the Eternal!" he commented, and according to all reports he was quite correct. The 2,500 mill workers were dressed alike in white muslin dresses tied with blue sashes. They carried parasols to protect them from the sun as well as to lend a proper note of decorum to the parade. The girls were grouped by departments, each led by its boss who carried a baton to indicate his authority. It took a half-hour for the procession to pass the President, after which the honored guest dined in the hotel while the workers were served a special banquet. Later in the afternoon the President was taken on a tour of the Merrimack Corporation's Mill No. 2, where the girls, still attired in their white dresses, stood at their machines to show how efficient they were on the job and what excellent working conditions they enjoyed.

Francis Cabot Lowell, an American who had studied English textile operations, designed one of the first practical power looms for making cotton cloth. He persuaded Nathan Appleton, a Boston banker, to invest $5,000 in a mill at Waltham, Massachusetts, and this proved so successful that Lowell sought another site where he could build a larger establishment. He found the perfect location at the junction of the Concord and Merrimack Rivers but died before the first mill opened in 1823. Lowell, for whom the new town was named, was interested in providing good living conditions for his employees, and his efforts at Waltham encouraged many other New England textile manufacturers to do the same.

Nathan Appleton and his associates influenced the development of the textile industry as they set the pattern for using cheap female labor, power machinery and a separate organization to sell the manufactured cotton goods. In addition to the Lowell mills, which were worth over $12,000,000 by 1840, Appleton also built up manufacturing centers in Lawrence, Massachusetts, and Manchester, New Hampshire. To him success meant not only profits but also good working conditions for the employees and, whenever possible, lower costs to consumers. Unlike the Rhode Island textile manufacturers, who induced whole families to come to work in their mills, the Massachusetts and New Hampshire industrialists depended mostly on young women for their labor force.

At Lowell the five-story red brick buildings, each topped

with a white cupola, were built along the river's edge. A large water wheel was installed in the basement of each structure, and through an intricate system of belts and pulleys it provided all the power required to run the many machines installed on the floors above. Close to the mills were red brick and white clapboard buildings that served as boardinghouses for the workers. The management felt responsible for taking care of its female operatives and acted not only as employer but as guardian and chaperone as well.

Each employee agreed to obey company rules, be in her house by a certain hour and always conduct herself like a lady. At night the young women were urged to improve their minds by listening to lectures, attending school or reading in the library. At one time the operatives wrote and published a magazine, *The Lowell Offering,* which gave those with literary inclinations the thrill of seeing their names in print. Many were so anxious to improve themselves that after working thirteen hours, they bothered to dress up and attend a two- or three-hour lecture or class session.

When these employees of the Merrimack Company or other textile concerns returned home for a visit or to marry, they told friends how they too might make money in the mills. Girls of that day could work either as domestics or as teachers, but textile mills presented new employment opportunities. When parents learned that the managements looked after their daughters and supervised their leisure hours, they had no qualms about letting them go. An operative made $1.50 a week (after paying for her board) and could always return home if she disliked or tired of her work. In a year or two she might save enough money for her dowry or for tuition to prepare for teaching.

Unfortunately, working conditions at Lowell and the neighboring mills were not quite as glamorous as President Jackson had been led to believe. The average working day was twelve hours, and as much as fourteen during the summer. The girls started work two hours before breakfast and were allowed thirty minutes for each meal. Much of the day was spent standing at machines, which proved tedious and physically tiring for some girls. When the mills first opened, the work was not hard and informality was the rule; but gradually as competition within the textile industry grew and production had to be increased, the machines demanded the girls' unflagging attention. Ventilation was inadequate because many foremen insisted on boarding up the windows to keep out the cold in winter and the dampness in summer. Whale oil lamps gave poor light and made the rooms stifling hot.

In 1834 the pretty, well-dressed Lowell girls decided they too wanted more money and staged a strike for higher wages. The ringleaders were fired and blacklisted and the other girls returned to work at their regular rate of pay. Later, other strikes were called, usually with the same results. Nevertheless, these strikes showed that the women were restive and aware that they were being exploited.

By 1842 newer and faster machines were introduced and a girl who was paid by piecework had no idle time on her hands if she hoped to make her $1.50 a week. When she could no longer keep pace with the speed-up and produce her quota, she had to leave.

The tide was changing in many ways. Girls were no longer voluntarily flocking to the mills. Instead, long black wagons called "black slavers" roamed through New England recruiting young women to operate the machines. When they arrived at the mills the girls were crowded into the boardinghouses and quickly put to work. Wages were often paid in store orders

20

rather than cash. Escape was no longer possible to many who wanted to quit their jobs because their families had abandoned their farms or moved on west. Thus many of the operatives had no place to go and were forced to remain in the mills.

Because of competition and with the price of textiles falling, it was necessary to cut costs in every possible way. The employees' welfare was forgotten as profits slipped, and the Lowell and other once-enlightened mills became less desirable places in which to work. Fortunately for the factory owners, immigrants were coming from Europe, and in 1848 a severe potato famine in Ireland caused thousands of young girls to immigrate to America. Many streaked to the mills, and by 1850 half of the operatives were Irish. With this abundant source of cheap labor, it was possible to continue operating the mills while paying starvation wages.

In an era when large numbers of women and children were forced to work in industry, the Lowell and a few of the other textile mills were temporary bright spots on what otherwise was a very gloomy horizon.

THE AGONY OF LABOR

Although there were a few humane employers like the early New England textile manufacturers and Joseph Bancroft in Wilmington, Delaware, most factory owners believed that labor was like any commodity that could be bought and sold. It was considered good business to hire men, women and children as cheaply as possible, make them work as hard as they could and, when they became inefficient, worn-out or unable to work for any reason, discharge them.

Let's pretend for a moment that it is sometime between 1820 and 1840, that you are living in the New England or Middle Atlantic states, and that your family is identified with the working class. If you are a girl, you may find work as a servant in a home or as a worker in a mill or small factory. With luck you may marry soon, be able to quit your job and have a home of your own.

If you are a man, probably you have been working since you were nine or ten. Now that you are married and the head of a family, you find that life can be most discouraging.

Your wages are probably as low as the factory manager dares make them. There seldom, if ever, is enough money to meet your expenses because living costs keep rising—but not your income. If your employer pays in store orders it costs you extra for everything you purchase at the company store.

Since you cannot afford to send your children to private school, there is little hope that they will receive an education, and you will find factory jobs for them as soon as they are old enough to work. If you are careless in managing your money you may find yourself in jail because you have incurred debts. Approximately 75,000 people go to prison every year, although half of them owe less than twenty dollars!

When it is time to serve your three- or four-day stint in the militia you will lose that much pay because, unlike the wealthy, you cannot afford to pay a fine that excuses you from the annual drill. If you are sick or injured on the job, your pay will stop immediately and you may be fired without notice or cause. If your employer fails or suddenly decides to go out of business and owes you back wages, you cannot collect them because mechanics' liens are not legal. Should you lead your fellow workmen in a strike for a living wage or shorter hours, the court will fine or imprison you for conspiracy.

As the country grows and business expands the merchant owners become more affluent and you find it increasingly difficult to make ends meet.

The large, multistory factory in which you work is a fire-trap, cold in winter, unbearably hot in summer. The machine you tend has no safety devices and the lighting is so inadequate that you cannot always see what you are doing. The pay may be poor but the hours are worse!

Here is how William Poole Bancroft described the working schedule for one of the better factories of the 1830's in the Wilmington, Delaware area:

During my boyhood and young manhood, the hours of work in the factory were 70 per week; and longer hours than that were usual in the cotton factories in the neighborhood. In summertime, when it was light enough ten minutes before five, we went to work at that time, and worked until 6 o'clock in the afternoon, being off half an hour for breakfast and 40 minutes for dinner. Nearly everyone lived close by, so we managed to get through in those short times for meals. On Saturdays, we stopped at 4 o'clock. This made up the 70 hours. When we could not see at ten minutes before five, we worked later in the evening. Other mills in the neighborhood worked about as long as they could see all summer. In winter, we got breakfast before going to work, started at 7, stopped at 8. During the short time in the spring and fall when we went to work before breakfast but could not see at ten minutes to five, we could not make our 70 hours and got behind in our time, but made it up working after 6 o'clock. I do not remember whether we ever worked after 8 in the winter-time; if so, it was only for a few minutes each night.

The craftsman was still far better off than the unskilled employee who worked on the docks or the roads, at manual labor or in the factories. The artisan's or mechanic's hours were long, but his wages were higher and his working conditions usually better than those of the laborer. It was easier for him to join with other members of his trade and make demands on his employer. Nevertheless, he too was anxious to shorten his workday and take home more money.

Employers were stanchly opposed to any unionization move on the part of their employees. They expressed regret at "the formation of any society that has a tendency to subvert good order, and coerce or molest those who have been industriously pursuing their avocation and honestly maintaining their families."

In the 1830's the courts still held that common law prohibited combinations and conspiracy in restraint of trade, and therefore strikes and labor unions were both illegal. It was held that the natural laws of supply and demand were the only legal ruling forces and should be allowed to take care of all such problems.

Under these conditions what could workingmen do with both employers and the courts arraigned against them? Their only hope was the fact that by 1830 most states had granted the vote to all white males. Would the workingmen, armed with votes, be able to win relief from the oppressive hours and low pay?

THE TEN-HOUR DAY

During the 1820's "sunrise to sunset" was the acceptable work schedule in most places. The first big break came in New York in 1828 when trade associations won a ten-hour day thanks to a shortage of skilled labor. New York thereafter became known as the "ten-hour town." As labor associations again sprang up during the 1830's the ten-hour day was one of the reforms they advocated.

One successful strike for the ten-hour day that never reached the courts was staged during the summer of 1835 in Philadelphia. Seventeen trade unions won support of the merchants, professional men and politicians for a strike that practically paralyzed the city. As the price for calling off the strike, employers granted the ten-hour day, and by the end of the year similiar strikes in other Middle Atlantic cities had won the ten-hour day for those strikers too.

By the middle of the century many states had enacted laws making it illegal for anyone to work more than ten hours a day. However, the legislation was not enforced. Employers circumvented the laws by refusing to hire anyone who would not agree to work longer hours, and except for most of the craftsmen the ten-hour day was still a dream.

THE WORKINGMEN'S PARTY

The large group of men was restless as it waited for the meeting to start. They had been called together on April 23, 1829, to determine what could be done to preserve the ten-hour day which the trade unions had just won in New York City. The threat of having to return to an eleven- or twelve-hour day was enough to galvanize everyone into action. Those who led the emergency meeting reasoned that if the craftsmen and mechanics joined forces with the unskilled laborers, all of them might elect their own representatives to the legislature. At last labor would have a voice in the government. A year earlier the first workingmen's party had been born in Philadelphia. The idea then spread quickly through Pennsylvania, jumped state lines into New York and New England.

The delegates attending this initial meeting in New York were so enthusiastic that they decided to broaden their objectives to cover other abuses inflicted on labor. Then they agreed to hold another meeting and invite all workingmen to attend. The second gathering attracted more than 6,000 who approved a statement setting forth what was felt were work-ingmen's rights. Next they delegated responsibility to a committee of fifty for seeing how this might be accomplished.

The committee's report was issued shortly and 20,000 copies distributed. It urged that a convention be called to nominate candidates for the New York Assembly from the ranks of labor, "who live by their own labour *And None Other*." Four days later the convention was held—after the hall had been cleared of all non-workers—and a slate of candidates was endorsed. It included a grocer, a printer, two mechanics and two carpenters.

The Workingmen's party received 6,000 votes out of 21,000 cast and elected Ebenezer Ford, one of the carpenters, to the assembly. Possibly the party would have done better had it not become dominated by several controversial and radical figures who gave it a dubious reputation and frightened the conservatives of that day.

One of the first bosses of the New York Workingmen's party was Thomas Skidmore, a machinist who had a fanatical devotion to the workers' cause. Self-educated, he did not believe in the right to own property. The long title to a short pamphlet he wrote in 1829 states this belief: "The Rights of Man to Property! Being a Proposition to Make it Equal among the Adults of the Present Generation; and to Provide for Its Equal Transmission to Every Individual of Each Succeeding Genera-tion, on Arriving at the Age of Maturity."

Skidmore hoped to lead workingmen in a revolt that would bring reforms. In the party's original platform Skidmore stated that "all human society, our own included as well as every other, is constructed radically wrong." He then proceeded to condemn the inheritance of wealth and the ownership of property. After this startling introduction the platform went on to demand the elimination of licensed monopolies, the enactment of mechanics' lien laws, the abolition of imprisonment for debt and the establishment of free education for all.

Skidmore's leadership quickly passed on to a group of English-born "free enquirers," George Henry Evans, Robert Dale Owen and Frances (Fanny) Wright.

George Evans was a printer who had founded the *Working Man's Advocate,* the official organ of the Workingmen's party. His newspaper gave labor its own press and espoused the workingmen's cause for several years. "All children are entitled to equal education; all adults to equal property; and all mankind, to equal privileges," the masthead stated. However, Evans mellowed over the years and later renounced Skidmore's radical ideas on property ownership in favor of a homestead law.

In 1827 Robert Owen and Fanny Wright had come to New York and established the *Free Enquirer,* a socialist publication. Owen, only twenty-eight, was a forceful speaker and an able writer. He opposed organized religion and favored a fairer distribution of wealth, less strict divorce laws and free public education. To promote democracy he wanted all children taken from their homes and brought up in national schools. "Thus may luxury, may pride, may ignorance be banished from among us, and we may become what fellow citizens ought to be, a nation of brothers," he wrote.

Fanny Wright, a tall, slender, good-looking woman, spoke out for women's rights, easy divorce laws and justice for the workingman. Upon arriving in the United States from Scotland, she established a colony at Nashoba, Tennessee, where she settled slaves whom she had purchased for liberation. When this project failed, she joined the cooperative community at New Harmony, Indiana, where Robert Owen's father had spent $200,000 trying to prove that his socialistic plans for replacing the factory system were workable. When this too failed, Miss Wright decided to join young Robert in founding the newspaper.

Owen snatched leadership of the Workingmen's party from Skidmore, whereupon the membership opposed his plan for having the state educate and bring up their children. Free public education, yes, but take the children away from their parents? Never! Furthermore they were not in favor of disturbing the present system of property ownership.

As a result the party broke into three groups and soon disappeared from the scene. Similar parties were organized in some eleven states, but all suffered the same fate. Workingmen's parties never had a chance. They were ridiculed by their opponents, who referred to them as levelers, a mob, a Derby Shirt party, ragtag and bobtail, ring-streaked and speckled rabble. Everywhere they were denounced by politicians and journalists.

Labor would have to find some other way to obtain justice!

VICTORY IN THE COURTS

"Here—take one and don't forget to come to the courtroom!" the baker said as he handed a circular to a passer-by. The man looked at the black picture of a coffin that headed the text and then proceeded to read:

On Monday, June 6, 1836, these Freemen are to receive their sentence, to gratify the hellish appetites of the Aristocracy. On Monday, the Liberty of the Workingmen will be interred! Judge Edwards is to chant the requiem! Go! Go! every Freeman, every Workingman, and hear the melancholy sound of the earth on the Coffin of Equality! Let the court-

28

room, the City Hall—yea, the whole Park, be filled with Mourners!

"What's this all about?" the man asked the baker.

"What! Didn't you know the jury found the journeymen tailors' society guilty of restraining trade? Are you going to stand still and let a judge condemn a man because he won't work for starvation wages? Why—even the New York *Evening Post* called it slavery!"

The other man asked what good it would do to crowd the court and make a commotion.

"You wait and see—we'll show that judge. If necessary we'll turn the town upside down and get rid of these laws."

The day of sentencing came, but the turnout of workers was disappointing. Another mass meeting was called a week later, and this time an estimated 27,000 people gathered, listened to speeches and hung the judge in effigy. The protest was not in vain, for it received such publicity that in two similar trials held shortly afterward, the juries decided the workingmen *not* guilty! This was progress, but so far no court had rejected the conspiracy doctrine.

Six years later, in 1842, a Massachusetts judge decided in the case of *Commonwealth v. Hunt* that it was not illegal for a union to strike for higher wages. At last the workingman had his first great victory—but although he was now free to strike that did not necessarily mean he would get what he wanted and in many cases deserved.

THE NATIONAL TRADES UNIONS

As the country expanded and trade increased between the states, the mill in New England found that it was competing with a similar business establishment in Pennsylvania. The

29

iron fabricator in Connecticut was in competition with a similar firm in Alabama. The Boston shoemaker no longer had the local market to himself, as nearby merchants stocked their shelves with boots made in New York, Philadelphia and a dozen other cities.

Labor had an interest in this development because for the first time what happened to workingmen in one part of the country affected those in another. The Boston shoemaker would have to take less money for his shoes—and perhaps cut his men's pay—if shoemakers in other cities slashed their prices.

In 1831 delegates from all over New England met in Providence, Rhode Island, to form the New England Association of Farmers, Mechanics and Other Workingmen. In 1834 the National Trades Union was established in New York City to include representatives from various city federations of labor. It backed the ten-hour day and the creation of still more trade associations, but the depression of 1837-1839 killed it and almost all the trade associations. It was not until the 1850's that national trade associations again were formed.

THE HOMESTEAD MOVEMENT

The depression of 1837 was especially severe. Factories closed, small businesses failed, thousands of workingmen were thrown out of work. The local, city-wide and national unions had little or no income and soon disappeared, leaving labor with no one to represent it.

During the 1840's there were many utopian experiments and ideas to which laboring people looked for economic help. Experimental colonies were established under the leadership of Robert Owen and other socialists, but these did not prove successful. George Henry Evans reappeared and in 1844 launched a campaign for free homesteads. He repeated again and again that strikes were futile, that wages were too low and that too much vacant property in the East was owned by speculators. If the land in the West could be opened up, he argued, enough people would move out there to bring about a labor shortage and a resultant increase in wages.

Horace Greeley (editor of the New York *Tribune*) and the editors of a few labor papers backed the idea of a homestead law, and in 1845 the first such legislation was introduced in Congress. Thereafter during the 1850's homesteading became a controversial political issue. The South feared that it would create additional antislavery states, and the eastern capitalists fought it because they believed their cheap labor supply would be drained off to the West. Once the Civil War broke out, the Republican party sought support from the growing landless class of workers, and with opposition from the East lessened, the law was passed in 1862. It provided that any person who was the head of a family or twenty-one years old, citizen, alien or loyal unionist, could enter a claim for 162 acres of public domain. He or she could take title to the land after it was occupied for five years and certain improvements were made on it.

Although thousands of people homesteaded, few of those trapped in the factories and mills could afford to go west, and the new law neither increased the wage rates nor reduced the working hours.

The factory system became a large and important part of the American economy during the first half of the nineteenth century. This happened partly because mass-production methods were adopted after Eli Whitney introduced into the manufacture of small arms the idea of standardizing parts and thus making them interchangeable in complicated products. By

1850 clocks, watches, locks, sewing machines, agricultural implements and many other things were being mass-produced in factories. Since such products could now be turned out by an unskilled machine operator, the American craftsman was bound to suffer. Although there was an ever-increasing number of unskilled factory workers, union activities continued to center almost exclusively about the craftsmen or skilled workers.

In the 1850's the union movement again gained momentum, and several national trade unions were founded. They were loose organizations with little or no power over their local affiliates. Nevertheless they gave workers experience in setting up this type of organization and helped train leaders for the conflict that was to come. During the Civil War the membership of labor unions grew, but these ineffective organizations failed to keep wages in line with the cost of living, and too often they antagonized employers, causing them to revive their antilabor associations and societies.

The Civil War freed the slaves but did nothing for the hundreds of thousands who were literally serfs in an economic system which still exploited labor for the benefit of those who had wealth, power or special privilege.

Little wonder that men gradually turned to violence in the struggle to gain their demands!

3

The Formative Years

THE KNIGHTS OF LABOR

IN AUGUST, 1866, SEVENTY-SEVEN TRADE UNION DELEGATES representing some 60,000 workers in thirteen states assembled in Baltimore and created the first permanent labor union, the National Labor Union. Perhaps its greatest contribution to the labor cause was its recommendation that unskilled workmen be organized into a "general workingmen's association" to be affiliated with it. Nothing came of the idea, however, nor was the organization successful in achieving an eight-hour day for its workers. Like their predecessors of the 1830's, the leaders of the National Labor Union became more interested in politics than in solving day-to-day labor problems, whereupon many trade unions withdrew. In 1872 the organization disbanded.

Meanwhile, some Philadelphia tailors under the leadership of Uriah S. Stephens established in 1869 the Noble Order of the Knights of Labor. Stephens, educated for the Baptist ministry, believed in building a "giant brotherhood of toil" that would embrace all mankind. Strikes and boycotts did not fit into his philosophy, and shortly after he became the first Grand Master Workman he resigned to enter politics. Terence V. Powderly took his place.

Unlike other labor organizations that operated in the open, Stephens insisted that this be a secret society to protect members from being fired or blacklisted for engaging in union activity. Only those who could give the correct passwords, pass grips and countersigns might attend meetings so that "no spy of the boss can find his way into the lodge room to betray his fellows." It was not until 1881 that the name and activities of the order were made public.

Anyone—man or woman—"working for wages, or who at any time worked for wages" was eligible to join. The Knights advocated many social reforms including an eight-hour day, equal pay for equal work, abolishment of child labor and also the establishment of cooperatives. Following the establishment of the original assembly of tailors, a second assembly made up of ship carpenters was founded in 1872, and soon many other local assemblies composed of carpenters, shoemakers, railroad men, miners and craft workers were started. As the movement spread, some assemblies signed up workers in various trades, and where there were not enough men of one craft to justify an assembly, a mixed group was formed, often including unskilled workers. District assemblies of delegates from the locals were provided, but it was not until 1878 that a National Assembly was established as the top authority.

Powderly, a short, slight man, had a varied business background that included practicing law, managing a grocery store, working as a railroad guard and a machinist. Essentially a humanitarian and a man of peace, he opposed strikes but was forced to support them although he felt that they were futile. Under his leadership membership in the Knights grew steadily but fluctuated greatly due to the failure of many strikes. Once a strike had been called off, members were usually blacklisted, unable to obtain work and therefore could no longer pay their dues. Unskilled workers could easily be replaced by strikebreakers, and the Knights were generally ineffective in conducting strikes of the craftsmen.

In 1885 the union achieved its greatest victory when railroad shopmen went on strike in the Southwest. For the first time labor forced the management of a large company to negotiate an agreement. Immediately workers all over the country clamored to join the Knights, and membership zoomed up from around 80,000 in 1885 to over 700,000 a year later.

The triumph did not last long, however, and May 4, 1886, proved a black day for the Knights. It marked not only the collapse of an unsuccessful railroad strike but the tragic riot in Chicago's Haymarket Square as well.

THE HAYMARKET RIOT

A cold drizzle began to fall that evening on Haymarket Square. It was May 4, 1886, and most of the crowd had slipped away into the night, leaving about 250 men gathered about the wagon where Samuel Fielden, an anarchist, was speaking about the insecurity of the laboring man and the abuses heaped on him.

"In conclusion . . ." He was about to end his speech, but at that instant a group of 180 policemen appeared in front of the wagon.

Captain Ward looked around at the small crowd and announced: "In the name of the people of the state of Illinois, I command this meeting immediately and peaceably to disperse." After a moment, during which no one moved, he pointed to those nearest him—"And I call upon you and you to assist."

"We are peaceable," Fielden insisted, as he and the other speakers prepared to leave the wagon. The meeting had been called to protest the brutal and unnecessary police killing of four strikers and the wounding of many others at the nearby McCormick factory the day before.

Suddenly a light sped through the air accompanied by a slight sputtering noise. The object crashed to the pavement by the first line of policemen, exploded with terrible fury, killed a Sergeant Degan and knocked down about sixty other policemen. For a few seconds all was quiet; then the uninjured police regrouped and charged at the fleeing crowd. A minute later the Haymarket riot was over except for the cries and moans of those who were hurt. Ten were dead, fifty were injured.

"Hang them first and try them afterward," many urged when they read the newspaper accounts of the riot. This advice was partly heeded, for Fielden, plus six innocent companions, received the death sentence. Four were executed, one committed suicide, two received long sentences but later were granted unconditional pardon. To much of the public this riot capped the climax of years of labor violence and strikes. From all sides came demands that something be done to stop the waves of irresponsibility and lawlessness.

Many people then had the impression that most workingmen were criminals who wanted to steal, kill, riot, burn property and overthrow the existing order. Some still remembered the great railroad strike of 1877 which brought outbreaks of violence and mob action, the miners' secret society called the Molly Maguires who terrorized the coal fields during a long strike, the textile strikes in the East, the steelworkers' strike of 1882, the many labor boycotts that swelled from thirty in 1884 to almost two hundred in 1885, and the wave of strikes that had recently spread throughout the country. Most frightening of all was the emergence in labor circles of a new anarchist element bent on revolutionary violence. It was not long before employers were adopting anti-union campaigns, courts were prosecuting union members for rioting and conspiracy, and state legislatures were passing laws that curbed activities of labor organizations.

After the Haymarket riot *John Swinton's Paper,* published in New York, stated that the bomb "was a godsend to the enemies of the labor movement. They have used it as an explosive against all the objects that the working people are bent upon accomplishing, and in defense of all the evils that capital is bent upon maintaining."

This unfortunate event, plus Powderly's bungling leadership and desire to reduce industrial strife, the failure of innumerable other strikes to win an eight-hour day, and a steady desertion by most of the skilled workers to form their own trade unions, quickly ended the Knights' influence as a significant labor organization.

SAMUEL GOMPERS AND THE A.F. OF L.

In 1863 Solomen Gompers and his family landed at Castle Garden in New York Harbor ready to take their share of the riches of the New World. His oldest son, Samuel, who was born in January, 1850, was a bright ambitious lad who knew what it meant to be poor and understood why his father had uprooted the family from London's slum of Spitalfields. There, from the age of six to ten, Samuel attended the Jewish Free School, but the family needed his help, so he left school to become apprenticed to a shoemaker. Dissatisfied with this work he apprenticed to a carpenter, attended night school and still found time for neighborhood social activities.

In their tenement flat on New York City's Houston Street life was no better for the Gompers than it had been back in Spitalfields. Although Samuel and his father were both busy making cigars at home, they could not earn enough money to support the family. Nevertheless, poverty did not keep young Samuel from again attending night school, sitting in on free lectures and joining various social clubs. At fourteen he joined the cigarmakers' union and at seventeen found employment in a factory where he immediately became active in the affairs of the local union. Shortly thereafter, his fellow employees selected him to be their spokesman to discuss grievances with their employer, and Samuel won the concessions they sought. The following year he married Sophia Julian, and as his family grew in size he found it increasingly difficult to support his wife and children. He had become concerned for the welfare of his fellow workers and gave so unselfishly of his time to the cause of unionism that he neglected his own well-being and that of his family.

The cigarmakers' union was weak and lacked leadership. Much of the work was done in tenements, labor-saving molds were being introduced, and other changes threatened the skilled worker as the depression of the 1870's reduced his wages. Late in 1875 Gompers teamed up with Adolph Strasser, another active union leader, to form a new local of which Gompers became president. Three years later they took over the Cigarmakers' International Union and instituted reforms that included uniform initiation dues, central control over strikes, equalization of funds among the various locals and establishment of a strike fund. Some 15,000 men joined, and although the union lost its first strike, it managed to feed the strikers, gaining experience and support. As a result of the strike, Gompers was blacklisted for four months, after which he threw himself into the union cause with even greater enthusiasm and turned his attention to the national labor movement.

In 1881, as a union delegate, he attended a meeting called in Pittsburgh to consider the creation of a new national organization which was named the Federation of Organized Trades and Labor Unions of the United States and Canada. Since it lacked a central headquarters, issued no charters and received no dues, the organization was weak and ineffective. Nevertheless, delegates met annually, and in 1884 one of the resolutions they adopted provided "that eight hours shall constitute a legal day's work from and after May 1, 1886." This provocative proclamation brought many recruits to the union, especially trade union Knights, because Terence Powderly opposed the short workday. Although thousands struck on May 1 for a shorter workday, the strategy failed and few won the concession. Undaunted, Gompers seized the opportunity to capitalize on the troubles besetting the Knights after the collapse of the southwestern railroad strike and the Haymarket riot. On December 8 of that same year a meeting was held at which the American Federation of Labor was formed, with Gompers its first president at an annual salary of $1,000.

The organization of the new A.F. of L. was based on the principal of craft autonomy—each organized craft to have its own constitution, rules and procedures for dealing with employers—rather than one big union with mixed assemblies made up of skilled and unskilled workers. For the next fifty years the A.F. of L. was to be the dominant, and sometimes the only, representative for organized craft workers. A good part of its success stemmed from Gompers' insistence on working for economic gains through collective bargaining with employers rather than engaging in political action, an activity which up to that time had usually proved disastrous to each new labor movement.

Gompers continued as president of the A.F. of L. (except for one year) until his death in 1924. A tireless worker, who in his later years associated freely with presidents, congressmen and Wall Street bankers, he nevertheless kept close to the rank and file workers, with whom he was proud to be associated. Ambitious, honest, always ready to make any personal sacrifice for labor's cause, and one who sought neither personal gain nor political favor, he died a poor man.

In his autobiography he stated: ". . . and I rejoice in the conviction that the bona fide trade union movement is the one great agency of the toiling masses to secure for them a better and higher standard of life and work."

Gompers' statement was sincere, but what of the masses of unskilled and unorganized workmen? It would be a decade after Gompers' death before anyone would come forward to help them organize.

JOHN MITCHELL AND THE U.M.W.

Since coal was first mined in this country emigrants from Great Britain had come in great numbers to dig beneath the ground. Most of the coal mined in the United States is bituminous, or soft coal, and smokes when burned. Anthracite, or hard coal, is found principally in the northeastern part of Pennsylvania and is mainly used for home heating because it is smokeless. Because the coal fields invariably were far from cities it was impossible for the men to change jobs readily. The mine operators provided housing and a company store, and the men had to pay whatever rents and prices the owners set.

40

Miners worked twelve to fifteen hours a day in unsafe and un-sanitary mines for a mere pittance, and were unable to do anything about their conditions.

In 1848 John Bates formed a union in Pennsylvania, and 5,000 men joined. A three-week strike ended in a compromise settlement, whereupon Bates disappeared and the union dis-solved. More immigrants poured in from Europe, many of them from Ireland, flooding the mines with surplus labor and making it hard for everyone to find jobs.

During the 1860's some scattered unions were organized, but the first effective unionization did not come until 1869 when, following a depression caused by overstocking of coal after the war, John Siney, an Irishman, organized a work stop-page which brought a sliding scale of wages. In 1873 he was elected president of the Miners' National Association. But during the next fifteen years other unions sprang up, the Knights enrolled many miners, and there was no single organi-zation to represent the miners and give them effective bargain-ing power. Finally, in January, 1890, the most important mine unions agreed to merge into a single union, and the United Mine Workers of America was formed under the American Federation of Labor.

One of the first presidents of the new union was John Mitch-ell. He knew how the miners lived, for he had been born in the mining town of Braidwood, Illinois, orphaned when six and reared by his stepmother, who took in washing. He had little time for school because he had to help at home, and at twelve he became a full-time miner. He joined the Knights of Labor, went west to work in various mines and returned home in 1888 to find not only that new immigrants had filled the mines but, worse, that wages had been cut 20 per cent. Disgusted with conditions he went west again in 1891, then

41

returned the following year and married Catherine O'Rourke. As he worked again in the mines he began to give serious thought to the miners' problems and how they might be remedied. He became secretary-treasurer of the northern Illinois subdistrict and in 1897 was appointed union legislative representative at Springfield, the state capital.

That July a national strike was called, but the southern Illinois miners did not participate, whereupon Mitchell was sent to organize the men. He did such a quick and effective job that his accomplishment came to the attention of the national officers. Meanwhile the strike ended in victory for the bituminous miners, as they won an eight-hour day, an extra ten cents per ton, standardization of screens and a differential between rates paid for run of the mine and screened coal. The following January when Mitchell attended the U.M.W.'s convention he was elected vice president, and the next year the miners promoted him to the office of president.

Only twenty-eight years old, the youthful chief executive of the United Mine Workers decided to visit some of the mines in outlying anthracite districts in eastern Pennsylvania in order to study working conditions at first hand. He had heard that they were bad, but he was not prepared for what he found. Italians, Slavs, Hungarians and other nationalities had been reduced almost to a condition of servitude. They lived in squalor, were overworked, underpaid, cheated when their coal was weighed and were victimized by the company's aptly named "pluck me" store. A congressional committee reported that some "hard-working, sober miners had toiled for years, and even a lifetime, without having been able to draw a single dollar or but a few cents of actual cash." These miners were divided by race, language, religion and suspicion of each other and saw no hope for the future. Native-born Americans despised and distrusted them because of their lower living standards and crude manners, and unions had passed them by, feeling it was hopeless to try to organize them.

As soon as the shy young man of twenty-eight took office he lost no time visiting the squalid hamlets of the oppressed anthracite miners. By enlisting support of the local priests, pastors and sympathetic civic leaders, by preaching the importance of unions and the brotherhood of man, by reminding the public that many of these men had not received a wage increase for twenty years, he soon won the support of the older miners and the trust of the younger immigrants. It took months of endless traveling, meetings, conferences and speeches before he felt confident that the men would rally with him.

After the mine operators ignored a call for a conference to negotiate benefits which the union wanted for its members, a strike was called, and all but 10,000 of the 140,000 miners threw down their picks and left their jobs. Mitchell worked feverishly to maintain their morale, insisting on good behavior and observance of the law. The operators granted some increases but ignored Mitchell and the union. The truce was an uneasy one, and when the contract expired in 1902, the men walked out again. This time the operators arrogantly refused to arbitrate. When the bituminous miners offered to call a sympathy strike Mitchell dissuaded them, believing that they could be of more help by contributing to a strike fund and preserving the dignity and prestige of the union. After six months of idleness Mitchell agreed to accept arbitration, and an Anthracite Coal Strike Commission was appointed, but without any member representing the miners! The following March the commission awarded the men a 10 per cent increase with a nine-hour day and established arbitration and conciliation boards but refused to recognize the union. Although

Mitchell accepted reluctantly he was hailed as a champion of labor and thereafter idolized by the miners.

Plagued by poor health, he yielded the presidency to Tom L. Lewis in 1907. During the ten years Mitchell served the union, it grew from 33,000 to 260,000 members and won decent wages and working conditions for both the bituminous and the anthracite miners. He spent his remaining years writing, teaching and working for the labor cause.

He died of pneumonia in 1919. "Champion of Liberty—Defender of Human Rights" was the epitaph that was chiseled on his tombstone.

4 ⊂⊒

The Betrayal of Labor

IN 1842 A YOUNG SCOTSMAN WHO HAD PREVIOUSLY BEEN A
cooper, or barrelmaker, arrived in Chicago to accept an ap-
pointment as the city's first detective. At the same time he
organized his own private detective bureau, which during the
next hundred years was destined to become one of organized
labor's foremost enemies. Allan Pinkerton had no use for the
common workingman, and his sympathies lay entirely with
the moneyed industrialists.

In 1861 he organized the United States Army's secret
service division and served as its chief until after the end of
the Civil War. During the postwar period he was extremely
successful in capturing bank and express thieves and recovering
stolen loot. The Pinkerton Agency became even better known
later for its strikebreaking activities, there being few major
industrial conflicts in which its detectives were not involved,
even as late as the 1930's. Hatred and fear of the organization
was expressed by the Populist party in its 1892 platform, which

45

called for elimination of many labor abuses including the "army of mercenaries known as the Pinkerton system." Although the company was hated, its methods were always legal, but sometimes of questionable morality. In an era when it was more popular to attack the workingman than help him, Pinkerton's behavior was no worse than that of the industrialists who contracted for his services. Upon his death a son, William Allan, took over the business, which gradually expanded into a nation-wide organization.

THE HOMESTEAD STRIKE

On the night of July 5, 1892, three hundred Pinkerton detectives armed with rifles marched aboard two barges anchored on the shore of the Ohio River below Pittsburgh. They were towed up the Ohio and Monongahela Rivers through the darkness to the Homestead plant of the Carnegie Steel Company situated opposite the southeastern part of Pittsburgh. They had been hired by Henry Clay Frick, the company's antilabor manager, to guard the property and enable it to import strikebreakers. The skilled steelworkers, who belonged to the powerful Amalgamated Association of Iron, Steel and Tin Workers, had agreed not to accept wage cuts and had walked off their jobs accompanied by the unorganized workers. Thereupon Frick had closed the plant and erected a high fence topped with barbed wire about the mills.

It was about four o'clock in the morning when the barges slowly approached the Homestead mills. When the hundreds of strikers crouching along the river bank by the steel plant saw the Pinkertons approach, they opened up with gunfire, hoping to drive the detectives away. For the next twelve hours shots were exchanged by the two "armies," and both sides suffered casualties. The strikers brought up a small cannon and fired it at the barges but failed to sink them. Later they rolled barrels of oil down to the river, emptied them on the water and set fire to the inflammable liquid. This trapped the Pinkertons, who now were jammed into one barge but with no tug to pull them to safety.

A white flag appeared above the vessel, and the Pinkertons agreed to discard their arms and ammunition in return for a guarantee of safe conduct out of town. When they came ashore, however, they were forced to run through the frenzied mob of strikers, who attacked them with stones and clubs before they reached the safety of a train that was waiting to take them into Pittsburgh.

There was an uneasy peace for a week until another army—this time 8,000 troops of the state militia—marched into town, declared martial law and surrounded the Carnegie Company's plant. Strikebreakers soon arrived, the strike leaders were charged with murder of the Pinkertons killed in the day-long battle, and the mill resumed production. By November, when the union conceded defeat, 2,000 strikebreakers were at work and only 800 of the 4,000 men who had gone out on strike were rehired.

Andrew Carnegie, who owned the plant, had previously stated that he was in favor of unions, and relations between the Amalgamated and the company had been good. Carnegie was in Europe at the time of the strike, having left Frick in complete charge of the business. Later, Carnegie admitted that Frick had his full support and approval in handling the affair as he did, although observers pointed out at the time that neither the company nor the union was justified in taking the law into its own hands.

The Homestead battle was one of the major skirmishes in the war between powerful unions and mighty corporations.

The incident provoked much discussion and concern, as some condemned management for using a private army of Pinkertons whenever it wanted to crush a strike, while others felt that a company had an obligation to work out a settlement with its employees. The prevailing belief was that the steel company had the right to protect those whom it hired and that it was justified in its action. As a result of the Homestead strike the Amalgamated union was smashed, and not until forty years later did the steelworkers have another strong union of their own.

EUGENE DEBS AND THE PULLMAN STRIKE

Pullman, Illinois, was a model town of brick houses and attractive flower beds which George R. Pullman, president of the Pullman Palace Car Company, had built for his 6,000 employees. His workers had no choice but to rent homes or apartments from the company and pay Pullman more for every service provided than it cost elsewhere.

The depression year of 1893 forced Pullman to lay off some 3,000 employees in September and cut the wages of those who remained by 25 per cent. Since rentals for company homes were not reduced, little was left from the average wage of six dollars a week after rent had been deducted. In spite of the depression, the company continued to pay dividends, and when it rehired the men who were laid off, it neither restored the wage cut nor lowered the rental charges.

In May, 1894, an employee committee asked for an interview with Pullman to discuss their grievances. He told them bluntly that the company was losing money and that the present scale of rentals must stand. Then, despite previous assurances to the contrary, three members of the committee who

48

belonged to the American Railway Union were suddenly fired. All the employees struck; Pullman locked the plant, considering their action disloyal, and decided to wait until the men were hungry enough to come back to work. Pullman was encouraged in his stand by the General Managers' Association, a group of railroad executives, for they were anxious to use this strike as a means of destroying the A.R.U., which had promised to aid the strikers.

The union was then only a year old, having been formed in June, 1893, by Eugene V. Debs, the former secretary-treasurer of the Brotherhood of Locomotive Firemen. Debs was born in Terre Haute, Indiana, in 1855, the son of French-Alsatian immigrants. When fourteen he obtained a job in the railroad shops and two years later became an engineer. At the age of twenty-five he was elected secretary-treasurer of the Brotherhood as well as editor of its magazine. During the next decade he was greatly responsible for the union's remarkable growth. In spite of his success in promoting the union, he became convinced that the only way to advance the welfare of all railway workers was to organize a single union rather than a few strong brotherhoods, each representing one craft or group. In 1892 he resigned from his job and set about organizing the American Railway Union.

Luck was with him, for when the unorganized workers of the Great Northern Railroad protested a wage cut and went on strike, they asked the new union to help them. Debs agreed reluctantly to organize the men and take over the strike, fearing that the union was too new to be of any great assistance. The railroad quickly capitulated, however, whereupon railroad men rushed to join the new union which grew within a year to a membership of 150,000.

Mindful of his success with the Great Northern and the impressive size of the A.R.U., Debs tried to arbitrate with Mr. Pullman, but the latter refused, asserting that there was nothing to arbitrate. Accordingly, June 26 was named by Debs as the date by which arbitration must be accepted or "the members of the American Railway Union shall refuse to handle Pullman cars and equipment on and after that date." The railroads fired every man who joined the strike, and soon some 60,000 men were out as railroad operations were disrupted in all parts of the country. The strikers did their best to avoid any violence or damage to property, and it looked as though they had a good chance to win.

They reckoned without U.S. Attorney General Richard Olney, to whom the General Managers' Association appealed for aid. Olney was a railway attorney who had served as a director of many roads. He asked President Grover Cleveland to assign troops to Chicago so that there would be no disruption to the mails and interstate commerce. The President replied that he would do this only if it were necessary to support a court order. By attaching mail cars to Pullman trains, Olney created a situation which made it necessary that a court injunction be issued ordering all persons "to refrain from interfering with or stopping any of the business of any of the railroads in Chicago engaged as common carriers."

Thereupon the force of deputy marshals was increased to a thousand, and when United States Marshal Arnold read the order to a crowd massed on the Rock Island Railroad's property at Blue Island (just south of Chicago) the men hooted and rough-handled both him and his deputies. Arnold immediately sent a wire to Washington, purposely exaggerating the situation, whereupon President Cleveland ordered the army stationed at Fort Sheridan to move into Chicago. With funds provided by the railroads, Arnold increased his force by 2,600 additional deputies whom the Chicago police called "thugs, thieves and ex-convicts."

The strikers and the crowds who gathered with them reacted by burning freight cars, signal towers, ties and freight awaiting shipment. By July 6 law and order seemed a thing of the past. Meanwhile Governor John Altgeld of Illinois (who recently had pardoned the anarchists imprisoned after the Haymarket riot) indignantly protested Cleveland's sending federal troops into Illinois without his approval. He ordered 5,000 of the state militia to Chicago to stop the rioting and burning. The arrival of these troops on July 7 only served to anger the crowds further. Strikers attacked one regiment which fired back killing and wounding several men. In the next two days, although more federal and state troops arrived to guard railroad property and patrol the streets, other incidents occurred.

Eugene Debs now asked the various trade unions in Chicago to start a sympathy strike, but they refused, awaiting the arrival of Samuel Gompers. When Gompers learned that there was no hope of victory for his rival union, the A.R.U., he refused to ask the railroads to take the strikers back without discrimination. With no one to plead their cause, the strikers suffered total defeat, the A.R.U. was badly weakened, its leaders were imprisoned and three years later the union dissolved itself.

Although many approved of Olney's action and the use of troops in the Pullman strike, there was much criticism expressed because he had resorted to the injunction and President Cleveland had brought in federal troops without permission of the governor. President Cleveland appointed a commission to investigate the whole affair, and its report later flayed the selfish paternalism of the Pullman Company and asserted that the railroad managers had acted wrongly but that the A.R.U. had not been guilty of provoking violence. Debs, who had been

51

arrested for contempt of court and for conspiracy, was sentenced to six months in jail. While there he became interested in socialism, read widely and later announced his conversion to the socialist cause as the best hope for labor. He later ran as the Socialist presidential candidate in five national elections.

As a result of the Homestead and Pullman strikes it became evident that labor was more than ever at the mercy of the employer. Not only could the boss hire the Pinkertons to guard his property and protect strikebreakers, but now he could go to court for an injunction to discipline strikers. Furthermore, as long as unskilled workers remained unorganized they could easily and cheaply be replaced with the endless supply of immigrants who came to the United States. Labor might protest but it could not fight the long hours, low wages and unfair practices. Many thoughtful men believed that the workingman's only hope lay in even greater development of trade unions rather than in unionization by industry, as was the aim of the A.R.U. This still left the unskilled worker without protection, but it looked for a time as though he might at last have a union of his own when the International Workers of the World was organized.

"BIG BILL" HAYWOOD AND THE I.W.W.

While the eastern miners under the leadership of the U.M.W. were making gains, the Western Federation of Miners withdrew from the A.F. of L. in 1897. For years those who settled in the West had shown an independent and sometimes lawless frontier spirit and were less inclined to agree to negotiation or arbitration than their eastern brothers. The miners of gold, silver, lead and copper fought a series of strikes that included killings, mob outbreaks, machine-gunning of union meetings, arrests, mine explosions, imprisonments and various other forms of violence. In the end they were defeated by the company guards, Pinkerton detectives and the law enforcement officers, who sided with the corporations. They therefore decided that the only way to win their demands was to form a broader and stronger organization that embraced many workingmen.

At a convention called by the Western Labor Union at Chicago in 1906, delegates representing many unions and political groups came with high hopes. One of them was Eugene Debs, leader of the Socialist party. Another was William D. Haywood of the Western Federation of Miners. Haywood, a towering stoop-shouldered giant with one eye, called the meeting to order and set the proper mood for the delegates by telling them that he believed violence was a necessary part of labor's struggle and that he favored direct action in dealing with labor problems.

Haywood, born in Salt Lake City, Utah, in 1869, became an orphan at three, and as a child was accidentally blinded in one eye. He started working at odd jobs when he was ten, entered the mines at fifteen and in time became a leader in the Western Federation of Miners. When the Federation organized the Western Labor Union to attract more members and help strengthen the general cause, Haywood became a member of the executive committee. Haywood believed that the revolutionary labor movement was the only way workers could win their emancipation from wage slavery. He was convinced that there would always be conflict between the working and capitalist classes and that therefore all laboring men would have to band together into a single organization.

It was due to the initiative of the American Labor Union that the Chicago convention was called. Here Haywood directed the deliberations in such a way that the delegates finally agreed to the establishment of a universal industrial union that would embrace all workers of the world. A platform for the new International Workers of the World was adopted which declared in part:

"The working class and the employing class have nothing in common. Between these two classes a struggle must go on until the workers of the world organize as a class, take possession of the earth and the machinery of production and abolish the wage system. . . . It is the historic mission of the working class to do away with capitalism. . . . An injury to one is an injury to all."

The convention had scarcely adjourned when the various delegates split into factions, and in 1906 a dispute between the moderate socialists and those who favored revolution caused many resignations. The next year the Western Federation of Miners, which had been responsible for founding the I.W.W., withdrew, leaving 6,000 members. A fight then broke out between those who believed the party should enter politics to obtain its objectives and those who thought it should use economic action. Those who urged political activity walked out, leaving only the men who said that the best way to help the working class was to overthrow capitalism through economic action that employed strikes, violence and sabotage when necessary.

The Wobblies, or "I Won't Work," as I.W.W. came to be called, found their greatest following among migratory harvest workers, mostly on the Pacific coast, lumbermen, western miners and construction gangs. The I.W.W. became synonymous with violence, but it was genuinely interested in helping unorganized and unskilled workers. The group was the first to employ the sit-down strike or slow-down, but the damaging reputation it gained for violence was perhaps not fully deserved. Its leaders were tireless zealots who went from strike to strike, helping the organizers, manning the picket lines, giving workers' families relief, agitating and stirring up trouble when they felt it would help the strikers' cause. They had both spirit and songs to buck up members' morale and give the rank and file a feeling of solidarity. Their songs were sung in the union meetings, on picket lines, at harvest camps, at hoboes' camps and wherever members of the I.W.W. gathered. "The Red Flag," "Dump the Bosses Off Your Back," "Are You a Wobbly?" "Paint 'er Red," and "Hallelujah I'm a Bum!" were among the best known.

The union probably won its greatest victory at Lawrence, Massachusetts, where the mill hands, mostly Poles, Lithuanians, Italians and Russians, made less than nine dollars a week and faced a drastic wage cut. Some 20,000 went on strike on January 12, 1912, and Joseph J. Ettor, a member of the I.W.W. general executive board, and Arturo Giovannitti, another I.W.W. leader, took over the direction of the strike. They arranged meetings of strikers, set up picket lines and distributed relief to needy families. Soon after the strike began, dynamite was discovered in various parts of the city, and the I.W.W. was immediately accused of being the culprit. The strike leaders denied any knowledge of the explosives, and later it was revealed that a local undertaker who hoped to sway public opinion against the strikers had been responsible. The head of the American Woolen Company was then arrested on charges of being implicated in the plot.

When the American Woolen Company tried to reopen the mills after refusing to discuss the workers' grievances there were clashes between police and strikers and an Italian woman was killed. Marshal law was declared, Ettor and Giovannitti were arrested and accused of being implicated in the woman's murder.

Now "Big Bill" Haywood arrived with other union workers to take charge. Surprisingly, Haywood insisted on an attitude of passive resistance rather than violence. Although police provided safe passage to the mills, the strikers stood by their picket lines and refused to return to work. As the strike continued into February, the problem of feeding the strikers' families became acute. In other cities sympathetic union members offered to provide homes for the children of parents on strike. As soon as several hundred youngsters had been rounded up and sent away, the president of the United Textile Workers accused the I.W.W. of trying "to keep up the agitation and further the propaganda of the Industrial Workers of the World." The authorities in Lawrence then announced that no more children would be permitted to leave.

Defying the police order, Haywood prepared to send another group to Philadelphia. The children were brought to the station, lined up two by two, and were about to be marched to the train when the police ". . . closed in on us with their clubs, beating right and left, with no thought of the children, who were in the most desperate danger of being trampled to death. The mothers and children were then rounded up and bodily dragged to a military truck and even then clubbed, irrespective of the cries of panic-stricken women and children . . ."—so stated the report of the Women's Committee of Philadelphia.

Protests poured in from every part of the country, and although there were more arrests and attacks on strikers, the men and women stayed on the picket lines until March 12, when the American Woolen Company capitulated. A government report sums up the strikers' gains:

Some 30,000 textile mill employees in Lawrence secured an increase of wages of from five to twenty per cent; increased compensation for overtime and reduction of the premium period from four weeks to two weeks. Also, in an indirect result of the Lawrence strike, material increases in wages were granted to thousands of employees in other textile mills throughout New England.

This victory brought national prestige to the I.W.W., and the following year organizers invaded Paterson, New Jersey, to help the silk weavers who were on strike. Although suffering from an ulcer, Haywood directed the strike, but the local authorities had no intention of letting the I.W.W. triumph here as they had in Lawrence. After five months of police brutality that included the usual breaking up of picket lines, clubbing of strikers—often into insensibility—and arrests on any pretense, hunger forced the strikers to return to work without winning any concessions from their employees.

When European hostilities broke out in 1914 the I.W.W. took a stand against war. The public labeled the union as unpatriotic and pro-German, and as soon as the United States entered the war, government agents broke into all offices of the I.W.W. and arrested its officers. Haywood and ninety-four others received jail sentences as high as twenty years. "Big Bill" skipped bail and fled to Russia, where he died in 1928. In 1919 the Communist party was organized in the United States and attracted many of the remaining Wobblies, and within a few years the union was all but forgotten.

THE PROGRESSIVE ERA

The period extending from the turn of the century to America's entrance into the first World War was known as the Progressive Era. This was a time when men and women were speaking out for an end to political corruption and for some protection from the practices of powerful economic interests.

Helping those who would reform the country were many authors who wrote "literature of exposure" and were nicknamed "muckrakers" by President Theodore Roosevelt. Among them were Ray Stannard Baker, Lincoln Steffens, David Graham Phillips and Ida M. Tarbell, who exposed the seamy side of American politics and business. Upton Sinclair's famous novel, *The Jungle,* told of the terrible working conditions and business practices in the meat-packing industry and brought quick corrective action. Some progressives believed that big business should be regulated in order to protect the workman, small businessman and the farmer.

One of the foremost progressive governors was John Peter Altgeld of Illinois, who was responsible for early labor legislation in that state. He appointed Florence Kelley of Chicago's Hull House as the first factory inspector, and in 1893 she obtained passage of a law which limited the working hours for women to forty-eight per week. Two years later the Illinois supreme court declared the act unconstitutional because it deprived each individual of the freedom to make a contract as guaranteed by the Fourteenth Amendment's "due process" clause. For the same reason in 1905 in *Lachner v. New York,* the United States Supreme Court ruled that a state law restricting working hours in bakeries was unconstitutional. Fortunately, the court reversed itself when it upheld Oregon's ten-hour law protecting women in business in the famous case of *Muller v. Oregon.* Following this decision many states gradually adopted industrial legislation for women as well as child labor, workmen's compensation and maximum hour laws.

In many states social workers and factory inspectors were pointing out the need for laws that would ensure safer and healthier working conditions in industry. The whole country awoke to just how bad conditions had become when, in 1911 on New York's East Side, 148 women lost their lives in the tragic Triangle Shirtwaist factory fire. The women were compelled to work in this sweatshop behind locked doors. This disaster helped focus attention on the problem of improving such conditions in industry and brought about much needed legislation.

In 1913 the Bureau of Labor was given cabinet status, and the following year Congress passed the Clayton Act, hailed by Samuel Gompers as labor's "Magna Carta." This strengthened previous antitrust laws and added significant sections which affected the rights of labor. "The labor of a human being is not a commodity or article of commerce," the law declared, as it made certain that antitrust laws should not be used to forbid the existence of unions. It also outlawed the use of injunctions in disputes between management and labor "unless necessary to prevent irreparable injury to property or to a property right . . . for which injury there is no adequate remedy at law."

With the declaration of war between the United States and Germany in 1917, labor pledged to aid the war effort, and in return for certain promises, President Wilson's administration granted labor most of the rights it had been demanding for so many years: the right to organize and bargain collectively, equal pay for equal work, the eight-hour day as far as possible, the right of all to a living wage.

Had the great day come at last? Had the victory been won— the victory for which so many labor leaders and workingmen had fought and waited so long?

In spite of the new laws, changed attitude of the courts and the Wilson administration's assurances, labor was still to be betrayed by most of the big corporations, which were as anti-union as ever and managed to keep a large part of their workers unorganized. Although during the war capital and labor observed a temporary truce, it was soon to end. Many corporations quickly showed a disposition to break any trust the workingman might have placed in them and to run roughshod over labor whenever it suited their best interests.

5

Decline of the Labor Movement

HEADLINES ON THE FRONT PAGES OF *The New York Times* for September 10–15, 1919:

BOSTON POLICE FORCE OUT ON STRIKE
MOBS SMASH WINDOWS AND LOOT STORES

TROOPS USE MACHINE GUNS ON BOSTON MOB
5000 GUARDING CITY AS RIOTS CONTINUE

BOSTON NOW FACES GENERAL STRIKE TO AID POLICE
FOUR MORE ARE KILLED, DAMAGE ESTIMATED AT $300,000
WILSON SAYS THE STRIKE IS A CRIME AGAINST CIVILIZATION

BOSTON POLICE VOTE TO RETURN TO DUTY
GOVERNOR MAY BAR THEM AS DESERTERS
WILL CONFER WITH UNION HEADS TODAY

BOSTON REFUSES TO TAKE BACK THE POLICE STRIKERS

61

The Boston police worked long hours and received salaries that started at $1,100 a year, inadequate to meet the steadily increasing cost of living. Although police were unionized in twenty-one cities, Edwin U. Curtis, Boston's police commissioner, believed that a police officer could not belong to a union and perform his sworn duty.

On September 9, 1919, at 5:45 P.M., 1,117 of the force's 1,544 men walked off their beats after some two dozen policemen had been suspended for joining the new A.F. of L. union. Reports of what happened are conflicting, but it appears that the state guard and volunteer police who were ready to patrol the city were purposely withheld so that lawlessness would occur and further incense the public against strikers. After Curtis fired the men he had previously suspended, Mr. Gompers telegraphed Governor Calvin Coolidge, complaining that the police commissioner's action was unwarranted. The governor replied that there was "no right to strike against the public safety by anybody, anywhere, anytime." Coolidge became a national hero, and there was general agreement that policemen were not justified in using the strike as a weapon.

This was only one of many strikes that swept the country after the end of World War I. During February of 1919 there had been a frightening general strike in Seattle that had crippled the city for four days. The strikers were called Bolsheviks and revolutionaries by the mayor, and he did his best to give the whole country the impression that this was the start of a dangerous revolutionary movement. Every day it seemed as though someone called still another strike, as the nation tried to adjust back to a peacetime economy.

Adding to the unrest was the emergence of militant labor leaders, some of whom had communistic (then often called bolshevik) leanings. The threat of communism was met head on by the American Legion, which preached "one hundred per cent Americanism." Legion members clashed with striking I.W.W. workers, socialists and others in the labor movement whom they felt were "un-American." Meanwhile the Ku Klux Klan, hooded bigots, whipped up hatred for Catholics, Jews and Negroes. Before this backdrop of class warfare, it was easy to turn public sentiment against labor unions and strikes, especially when many of the workers involved were of European origin, unable to speak English and suspected of being revolutionists.

THE GREAT STEEL TRAGEDY

As soon as the Boston police strike left page one of the newspapers, the steel companies took even bigger and blacker headlines. It was little wonder that trouble was brewing there. A strong union in the steel industry had been crushed years before, and now half of the men still worked twelve hours a day, seven days a week, and sixty-nine hours was the average workweek. Anti-union spies roamed the mills and reported any signs of labor agitation. This was too large and important an industry for labor leaders to ignore, and by 1918 the A.F. of L. decided it was time to organize the steelworkers. They chose William Z. Foster for this important job.

Foster, a former railroad carman, became a left-wing socialist and joined the I.W.W. in 1909. Two years later, while traveling through Europe as a correspondent for the I.W.W., he changed his ideas. Instead of backing a radical union to compete with regular trade unions, he now believed that the

I.W.W. should become a propaganda organization that would start "boring from within." During World War I Foster severed all his radical connections and worked hard for the government's Liberty Bond Drive. Thus when the A.F. of L. looked for someone to organize the steel industry, he appeared a likely candidate and was chosen to spearhead the drive.

At his suggestion representatives of various interested international unions were invited to a meeting and formed a National Committee for the organizing of the Iron and Steel Industry. Foster was elected its secretary. The organizing campaign opened in 1918 and was an immediate success. Steelworkers rushed to sign up with the union. However, repressive measures were taken against workers, and most of those who joined the union were fired. Steel management refused to meet with the labor leaders, and with more and more men being fired for joining the union there was nothing for Foster to do but order a walkout. A strike was set for September 22, 1919. President Wilson asked Foster to rescind the strike order, but he refused to back down and 343,000 men quit their jobs. In many Pennsylvania towns union meetings were forbidden, and police expelled organizers from mill towns. In one instance they broke up an organization meeting and in the excitement a woman was brutally killed.

The strike affected most steel-producing plants and shut every mill. Immediately clashes broke out between the strikers and police, their deputies and company guards, as it became evident that the steel companies were not going to recognize the strike and would do everything in their power to break it. Advertisements appeared in leading newspapers telling the steel companies' position, and most of the news stories were slanted against the steelworkers who were described as radical foreigners.

The Foremen's Association of the National Tube Company's Elwood Works circulated a poster through the mills that read:

WAKE UP, AMERICANS

ITALIAN LABORERS, organized under the American Federation of Labor, are going to strike Monday and are threatening workmen who want to continue working.

These foreigners have been told by labor agitators that, if they would join the union, they would get Americans' jobs.

They are encouraged by ITALIAN MERCHANTS who are in sympathy with them.

ARE YOU GOING TO SLEEP AND LET MOB RULE THREATEN THE PEACE OF OUR TOWN?

Violence was rampant in the mill towns. When the Reverend Kazencz dismissed his congregation from the Temple of God at Braddock, Pennsylvania, police charged into the midst of parishioners coming from the church. They were forced to run for their lives. State troopers were dispatched to Gary, Indiana, when Negroes were brought in by the steel company as strike-breakers. A fight between strikers and police resulted in twenty deaths, eighteen of them strikers. As thousands of strike-breakers arrived at the mills, police charged through picket lines, broke into union meetings and harassed the strikers in every possible way. Civil liberties were suspended in many communities as local and state police, together with their deputies, attacked the strikers.

Early in October the Industrial Relations Department of the International World Movement, a Protestant church organization, appointed a special commission of inquiry to look into the strike and try to bring the parties together. By now every sign indicated that the strike had been broken. The steel companies were gradually restoring operations, and many regular workers who were afraid of losing their jobs permanently to the strikebreakers deserted the picket line and returned to work.

On December 5 Judge Gary, head of the United States Steel Corporation, declined mediation efforts of the commission of inquiry on the ground that the men still out were bolshevist radicals who were not wanted in the mills and would not be taken back. On the twentieth of the month he refused to meet with union leaders, and as the strike dragged on so many men had claimed their old jobs that in January, 1920, the strike was abandoned. Those men who were not yet blacklisted crept back to their jobs and the same conditions they had left.

In a final report the commission of inquiry, which supported the workers, declared that the United States Steel Corporation was too large and rich to be beaten by 300,000 workingmen. It had too many allies in business, government, the press and the pulpit to be defeated by widely scattered workers under an improvised leadership. Among its many findings was one letter of instructions sent by a company to its agents. It read:

"We want you to stir up as much bad feeling as you possibly can between the Serbians and Italians. . . . Call up every question you can in reference to racial hatred between their two nationalities."

It would be almost two decades before union leaders made another attempt to invade the industry and unionize its workers. Meanwhile the men learned to live with the conditions as best they could. However, three weeks after the strike ended, lower-paid employees received a 10 per cent increase, and in 1923 the industry abolished the twelve-hour shift. Perhaps the strike had not been altogether in vain!

JOHN L. LEWIS AND THE U.M.W.

After the collapse of the steel strike the United Mine Workers were the next to capture the front-page headlines as 435,000 men came out of the ground to form picket lines around their mine entrances. They wanted a 60 per cent wage increase, a six-hour day and a five-day week. This thirty-hour workweek, the idea of their new young president, John L. Lewis, was his way of spreading work in an industry whose production would be cut back now that the war was over.

President Wilson declared the strike "morally and legally wrong." In spite of a previous pledge not to use court injunctions to stop strikes, the President ordered such an action brought against the U.M.W. to restrain all officers of the union from carrying on strike activities.

"We cannot fight the government," Lewis said. He canceled the strike order but the miners refused to obey him. It was his first test of strength, and he managed to work out a compromise that gave the men a 27 per cent pay increase with no reduction in hours. Just as Coolidge had gained stature and political strength from the police strike, so did Lewis' handling of the miners' strike enhance his position with the union members.

John Llewellyn Lewis was born February 12, 1880, at Lucas, Iowa, where he grew up in an insecure home, for his father, who was a miner, knew what it meant to be blacklisted for holding a union card. After attending elementary school he went to work and then entered the mines, but when he turned twenty-one he began four years of travel through the West, working at many jobs, chiefly mining. He returned to Lucas, married Myrta Edith Bell and served as a delegate of a Lucas mine to the national convention of the United Mine Workers.

In 1909 he moved to Panama, Illinois, was elected president

67

of the local union, and in 1910 became the union's state legislative representative. The following year Samuel Gompers met him and was so favorably impressed with the tall, muscular, young man that he hired him as a field representative of the A.F. of L. In 1917 Lewis returned to the U.M.W. as its statistician, then quickly rose to become vice president, acting president and finally in 1920 its president.

The vigorous new executive sought to organize the southern mines to protect northern wage scales, and this met with angry resistance from the operators who were in no position to grant wage increases or other benefits while prices were falling. In April, 1922, the bituminous coal contract expired, and 500,000 men walked off their jobs followed by 150,000 anthracite miners. It was during this strike that one of the most brutal cases of labor violence took place at Herrin, Illinois.

On June 21 the Southern Illinois Coal Company, which had recognized the U.M.W. before the strike, hired men from another union. Some of the miners tried to talk with the strikebreakers, but machine guns kept them at a distance and killed two of their number. The company then brought Hargreaves Secret Service operatives from Chicago to guard the coal field, which was being worked with a steam shovel from above the ground. Although a stockade had been erected about the area, hostilities broke out and three guards were shot.

Tension and anger now mounted throughout the countryside as men in Herrin, West Frankfort and other nearby towns feared for their jobs. Mobs broke into stores and quickly seized all available arms and other weapons and surrounded the stockade. The guards fired at the strikers, who returned the shots and prepared to storm the barricade. An armistice was then negotiated, it being agreed that the strikebreakers and guards would be permitted to leave the mine property safely, provided they returned home. White flags were raised by each side indicating acceptance of the truce.

As the strikebreakers, guards and managers of the mine marched from the stockade in groups, they were led away from the road and treacherously attacked by some of the strikers who were crazed by fury and a desire for revenge. Nineteen of the strikebreakers were murdered, two strikers were killed and many were injured. The nation was shocked by this barbarism. President Warren G. Harding denounced the killings and bolstered the fight for open shops, saying, "A free American has the right to labor without any other's leave." Meanwhile, no immediate arrests were made at Herrin; villagers gave alibis for those union members accused of murder, the U.M.W. contributed liberally to the men's defense and two juries exonerated the miners who had been accused of the murders.

Lewis and the U.M.W. eventually gained certain concessions before the strike was called off, but the general cause of labor suffered a setback from the brutal massacre. Enemies of labor seized on the Herrin affair as one more reason for adopting the "American Plan."

THE AMERICAN PLAN

The general resentment which business leaders felt toward the labor movement inspired a campaign during the early 1920's which called for the open shop. The open shop affirms the right of the employer to hire whomever he wishes whether or not an employee belongs to a union. Actually, experience had already shown it to be a means by which an employer could discriminate against a union even though the majority of his employees were members, because at that time in an open shop no group of workers could force an employer to engage in collective bargaining.

"American Plan" was the patriotic name given to this principle. Groups of businessmen who advocated the open shop organized throughout the country while chambers of commerce, manufacturers' associations, the National Metal Trades Association, the National Association of Manufacturers and other business organizations supported the movement.

The Bethlehem Steel Corporation not only adopted the open-shop policy within the company but refused to sell steel to builders who did not adhere to the principle. Referring to Eugene Grace, president of the Bethlehem Steel Company, the New York *World* said: ". . . that he, personally, the Bethlehem Steel Company, the Bethlehem subsidiaries, and practically all the steel interests of the country are endeavoring to kill off union labor and create non-union shops if human ingenuity can do it."

The meat packers in Chicago canceled their union agreement and established an open shop. Many building trade unions, textile unions and newer wartime unions were victims. A railroad strike in 1922 ended with the re-establishment of the open shop on several lines. As the American Plan spread, union membership declined; and once the open shop returned, back came the "yellow dog" contracts, which prohibited employees from joining labor unions, and back came company unions, company labor spies and company policing in many plants.

All was not hopeless, however. The 1920's brought mass production to the factories and increased employment in industrial plants. Although business was generally unfriendly to the labor union, it nevertheless felt and expressed a concern for the welfare of the workingman. Many firms introduced employee benefits such as health, accident and life insurance, educational and health service plans, recreational facilities, employee stock ownership plans and company-run cafeterias. Unfortunately, the provisions and conditions of all employee welfare plans were decided upon by the employers, not by labor.

Although efforts to abolish child labor were attacked by business interests as "socialism" and invasion of states' rights, certain advances were made. The same objections assailed legislation aimed at further improving working conditions for women. With the nation's economy prospering, business was clearly in the saddle, and it had no intention of changing the social order.

The A.F. of L. placed great emphasis on labor-management cooperation and, satisfied with the gains its skilled members were making, made no effort to widen its activities. Wages in general rose during the 1920's and there was improvement in the hours of work. This was, however, a period of labor-management cooperation rather than collective bargaining, and employees depended upon their employers' good will for such new benefits as they received.

During the late 1920's there were warnings of an impending economic crisis if nothing were done to stop the mad inflationary boom. Through 1928 and 1929 prices on the New York Stock Exchange kept rising until Thursday, October 24, 1929, when suddenly the bull market broke as thousands of frightened speculators sought to sell their stock. Bankers tried to restore confidence by buying securities but it was too late. The boom was dead.

NOTHING TO FEAR!

The effects of the stock market crash in October, 1929,

were not felt immediately. During 1930 less than 10 per cent of the big corporations reduced wages, although some smaller concerns started slashing salaries and work forces early in the year. By the end of 1930 unemployment was estimated to have risen to between 3,000,000 and 6,000,000, and it kept leaping higher as bad business conditions forced more and more companies to retrench or close up altogether.

The only bright spot on the horizon for labor was the Norris-La Guardia Act of 1932. Since 1880 the courts had supported employer "yellow dog" contracts. Such contracts were found throughout much of the mining industry and were used successfully to keep industrial workers from unionizing. Skilled workers, however, who belonged to strong craft unions, refused to sign such contracts. The Norris-La Guardia Act not only forbade "yellow dog" contracts but also greatly limited the power of federal courts to use injunctions in labor disputes.

As the depression deepened more than 14,000,000 Americans were unable to find jobs. For these men and women and millions of others there was no hope until 1932 when Franklin Delano Roosevelt launched his presidential campaign with the fighting promise: "I pledge you, I pledge myself to a new deal for the American people." Swayed by his optimism and confidence that the Democratic party would bring back prosperity, the voters sent him into the White House with a tremendous popular vote.

Saturday, March 4, 1933, was a dreary, cold day, a bitter disappointment to those in charge of the presidential inauguration ceremonies in the nation's capital. There was something almost symbolic about the weather, for it seemed to match the mood and misery of the whole country.

By this time there was hardly a state in which some banks were not closed or partially shut. In Indiana withdrawals were limited to 5 per cent of a depositor's bank balance as of February 25. A new law in Pennsylvania required depositors to document the reasons for their withdrawals. That very morning Governor Lehman of New York had at last reluctantly declared a two-day holiday in the Empire State.

The banking crisis was not the only problem that faced Franklin D. Roosevelt that noon as he took his oath of office. Throughout the nation countless factories and offices had closed. Thousands were hungry, many were destitute and without hope. In one state several hundred hunger marchers had just descended on the legislature demanding cash relief.

"We want work! We want work!" they chanted in unison at the bewildered lawmakers.

The city of Newark, New Jersey, had no money to meet its payrolls. A moratorium had been declared on foreclosing personal property or realty mortgages in Iowa. Slowly but surely the economic life of the nation was grinding to a halt.

"There is nothing to fear but fear itself," President Roosevelt told the throng before him and the untold millions gathered about their radios. *Nothing to fear*—when the country's economic system faced collapse, when people were homeless, jobless, starving! It took courage to speak those words, and that day the New Deal and new hope for America were born.

6

Government and the Workingman

It was September 13, 1933, and New York's Fifth Avenue had never seen anything like it! More than a quarter of a million employees and their employers were organized into seventy-seven trade and industry divisions to march before a million and a half spectators. From one thirty in the afternoon until midnight they passed the reviewing stand—clerks, dressmakers, office boys, Paramount Theater girls costumed like blue eagles, bankers, municipal workers, chorus girls, young men of the Civilian Conservation Corps dressed in olive uniforms, brewers, mechanics, waitresses, salesmen—people from every segment of business and industry. They marched more than four miles to the music of hundreds of bands and the roar of airplanes overhead, all to show President Roosevelt and the N.R.A. (National Recovery Administration) that they were behind the Blue Eagle—the symbol of the N.R.A.

"The most amazing thing about the outpouring of industry is the spirit of determination shown on the face of every

74

marcher," Grover Whalen, New York's N.R.A. administrator, observed. "It shows that they are determined to end the depression by enlisting under the banner of the N.R.A. and marching with President Roosevelt to a new and better day."

The hope and confidence Grover Whalen saw in the marchers' faces were contagious. Those on the sidewalks as well as the millions who watched similar N.R.A. parades in other cities felt it too. At last something had happened! Instead of holding endless hearings and investigations, the government was taking positive action to pull the country out of the depression. President Roosevelt had said "nobody is going to starve," and here was proof he meant what he said. There would be employment for all, fair wages, good working conditions and once more the American economy would hum at full speed.

President Roosevelt came from a wealthy family, but this did not prevent him from understanding and sympathizing with the plight of the "have nots." Perhaps the fact that he always had so much made him particularly aware of the needs of those who had so little. It may have been that his long illness and fight to recover from crippling polio had made him sensitive to the suffering of others. Not only did he radiate his warmth and concern for the welfare of others but he also loved people as individuals, and he was anxious to have them love him too. Roosevelt thought he knew what people wanted and needed and was not afraid to fight so they might have economic and social justice. His goal was to raise living standards permanently, not by taking away from the rich but by helping those who had little or nothing.

The National Industrial Recovery Act (N.I.R.A.), signed on June 16, 1933, was one of the many important laws Congress passed during those historic, hectic, early days of the

75

New Deal. Its purpose was to start the wheels of business spinning again by eliminating cutthroat competition and overproduction by "self-regulation" through industry codes. At the same time prices would be raised so that a reasonable profit could be earned. Millions of workingmen would be protected by guarantees of a minimum wage, generally between thirty and forty cents an hour or fifteen dollars a week, reasonable hours of work and the right to collective bargaining. The law provided that each division of commerce and industry would have a committee representing labor, management and the public, to draw up and adopt a code which would be observed by all who signed it. Each company that signed was given a Blue Eagle emblem to display in its place of business. To get the program started $3,300,000,000 was appropriated for a public works program to stimulate the economy and get men working again.

One of the most famous provisions of the N.I.R.A. was Section 7(a). This provided that every N.R.A. industrial code drafted by a committee and signed by a business firm should contain these three important provisions:

(1) That employees could organize and bargain collectively through their own chosen representatives without any interference;

(2) That no new employee could be prevented from joining a labor union of his own choice or be compelled to join a company union; and

(3) That employers must pay the minimum wage rates and comply with maximum hours of work and other conditions of employment as set forth in the code adopted by the industry.

Section 7(a) was a major victory for the laboring man. President Roosevelt called it "the most important and far-reaching legislation ever enacted by the American Congress."

This was a real turning point for labor because as William Green of the A.F. of L. said, it would give millions of workers "their charter of industrial freedom."

REBIRTH OF THE LABOR MOVEMENT

One of the most significant results of the N.I.R.A. was that Section 7(a) filled labor leaders with renewed enthusiasm. They lost no time planning intensive membership recruiting programs. Organizers rushed out to revive dead local unions, start new ones and move into areas where they formerly were forbidden. Miners arriving at work saw signs which said: "President Roosevelt wants you to join the union." A few months later the United Mine Workers had signed up 300,000 new members and negotiated agreements in the non-union coal fields of Alabama and Kentucky.

President Green confidently predicted that the A.F. of L. union would attain its goal of 10,000,000 members and someday grow to 25,000,000. Actually its membership soared from 2,137,000 to 3,045,000 between 1933 and 1935, and the ranks of all unions increased by almost a million members.

The initial enthusiasm was short-lived, however. The N.I.R.A. could not immediately change long-standing prejudices and ways of doing business. Despite the codes they had signed, many companies were determined to resist unionization, and thousands of employers defied the N.R.A. in labor disputes and took their cases to the courts. The coal and steel industries refused to sign until pressure was brought on them, and Henry Ford would not become a party to the automobile code because many of the manufacturers from whom he purchased parts were not under codes and he was against the principle of the N.R.A. anyway.

Labor was able to resist. The law was on its side even though Congress had failed to provide proper machinery to enforce Section 7(a). Heartened by the legislation, men and women sought to win what should now be theirs legally, and they showed that they were ready to use their only weapon—the strike—to get it.

The first strike that took place under the N.R.A. was at Uniontown, Pennsylvania, when the W. J. Rainey Company discharged two members of workmen's representation committees. Elsewhere, at Lodi, New Jersey, dye workers were routed by tear gas. Upstate New York milk producers, who received one and a half cents a quart for their milk, battled with troopers as they tried to stop milk deliveries. At Armridge, Pennsylvania, 200 armed deputies attacked a crowd of pickets with bullets and tear gas, killing one man and wounding dozens. By September more than 100,000 workers in the coal, steel and automobile industries were out on strike and clashing continually with the police. All told, during 1933 there were 1,667 strikes that cost wage earners more than $54,000,000.

Things were not much better the following year as both the number of strikes and the violence increased. In July one of the most terrifying and spectacular strikes occurred in San Francisco. The city was completely paralyzed for a whole day by a general strike. A quarrel between longshoremen and their employers grew into a general labor walkout of all industry and services. With the arrival of General Hugh Johnson, who headed the N.R.A., the strike collapsed quickly.

The climax was still to come when a month later the largest single strike in the history of our country spread through twenty states.

78

THE GREAT TEXTILE STRIKE OF 1934

Representatives of the cotton garment industry gathered from all parts of the country on August 27, 1934, and adopted a resolution which refused to obey the recent order of President Roosevelt reducing hours of work and raising wages for 250,000 workers in the industry. The order affected 4,000 units in forty-two states. In voting to defy the President's order the manufacturers called it "unjustifiable, unwarranted, burdensome and inequitable."

Four days later the United Textile Workers issued strike orders to 1,000,000 employees in the cotton, wool and silk industries. The union demanded for its membership recognition of the union, abolition of the stretch-out and speed-up and a thirty-hour workweek with no reduction in the minimum fourteen dollars a week wage. The textile industry had been sick for some time, but union officials did not believe that this excused the companies' willfully flouting the textile code.

Within a few days it was feared that the strike would spread to other industries too. Already 110,000 textile workers in Massachusetts were on strike. In Rhode Island 50,000 had walked off their jobs, in Georgia 60,000 and in Alabama 28,000. Altogether about half a million men and women were idle. It was the biggest strike the country had ever seen!

The governors of eight states had called out the National Guard to preserve order. Governor Francis Green of Rhode Island summoned the legislature into extraordinary session to request federal troops to assist the National Guardsmen.

"We are face to face now not with a textile strike," he said gravely, "but with a Communist uprising."

The state senators backed him but members of the House evidently did not believe that the Communists were responsible for the strikes or that the situation was out of hand. After Governor Green talked with President Roosevelt, he too decided that the crisis had passed.

On September 21 the executive committee of the textile union agreed to call off the strike after President Roosevelt appointed a committee headed by Governor John Winant of New Hampshire to study the problem and make recommendations. Following virtually continuous sessions for twelve days, Governor Winant presented his committee's "peace treaty," which made numerous suggestions for settling the dispute but actually left matters exactly where they had been before the strike was called.

The striking textile workers returned to the same working conditions that they had asserted were intolerable three weeks before. Their only hope was that employers would agree to the spirit of the Winant report or that the government would obtain power to enforce its provisions.

No such thing happened. Instead, approximately 80,000 workers in the South found 200 mill gates closed when they returned to work. Many in New England charged that their employers discriminated against them as they sought to recapture their former jobs. Worse still, numerous employers who had made every effort before the strike to carry on in spite of bad business conditions now felt little or no obligation to provide further employment.

All hope was gone for the textile workers. Half a million of them had sacrificed up to three weeks precious wages; many of them lost their jobs; and several hundred thousand workers who had confidently joined the ranks of the United Textile Workers during the strike soon deserted it. Little wonder the workers were disillusioned and bitter.

BLACK MONDAY

The year 1934 spelled defeat for labor. In spite of minor local successes, in the mass-production industries workmen failed to win their rights under the N.I.R.A. In September President Roosevelt asked General Johnson to resign and abolished the office of National Recovery Administrator. Concurrently he created the National Industrial Recovery Board, which was to consist of representatives from management, labor and the public. The new board was independent of the N.R.A. but it inherited two problems from the National Labor Board which it succeeded. There was no effective way of enforcing its decisions, and it still kept the principle of "majority rule," which held that if a majority of workers chose a union, the employer must bargain exclusively with the union as though it represented all the workers.

The board failed to win the confidence of either labor or management. To enforce its decisions it had to depend upon the N.R.A. to withdraw the Blue Eagle from an offending employer (which the N.R.A. did not always do), or it had to ask the Department of Justice to bring legal action against the offender.

Appearing before a Senate committee, Francis Biddle, chairman of the National Labor Relations Board, declared that "the recommendation of the National Board is nothing more than an opinion." Its members concluded: "The board is powerless to enforce its decisions."

Events moved swiftly toward a showdown during the first part of 1935.

In January the Supreme Court ruled that Section 9(c) of the N.I.R.A. unconstitutionally gave the President legislative power to regulate the petroleum industry.

In February a federal district court found in the Wierton

81

case that Section 7(a) of the N.I.R.A. was unconstitutional.

By March little or no action had been taken on the thirty-three cases which the National Labor Relations Board had referred to the Department of Justice for prosecution.

Then the final blow struck. On "Black Monday," May 25, the Supreme Court declared in the Schechter poultry case that the N.I.R.A. was unconstitutional. Business hailed the decision because it ended the government's authority to regulate the economy and it removed the necessity for industry to bargain collectively with its employees, something that most businessmen hated.

As for labor—the workingman would again be without true representation, still not free to organize or enjoy collective bargaining. That night there was gloom in every labor camp.

THE WAGNER ACT

In March of 1934 Senator Robert Wagner had introduced a bill which retained and tightened Section 7(a) of the N.I.R.A. President Roosevelt had asked him to withdraw it temporarily until the N.I.R.A. had been given a fair trial. The senator complied with the President's request, but when it became apparent that the N.I.R.A. was a failure, he reintroduced it in 1935, and less than two weeks before the Supreme Court killed the N.I.R.A. the Wagner bill passed the Senate.

The House of Representatives received the bill, and labor leaders demanded its immediate approval. President Green, in testifying before a congressional committee, said:

"I do not mind telling you, that the spirit of the workers in America has been aroused. They are going to find a way to bargain collectively. . . . We cannot and will not continue to urge workers to have patience unless the Wagner bill is made law, and unless it is enforced, once it becomes law."

President Roosevelt had no intention of letting labor down and immediately supported the bill, which was passed, and he signed it into law on July 5, 1935.

The Wagner Act, often called the cornerstone of President Roosevelt's labor program, reaffirmed the principles of the now dead Section 7(a) of the N.I.R.A. Not only did it give the new National Labor Relations Board power to issue cease and desist orders that would compel employers to obey the law, but it also provided machinery so that the board could enforce its rulings. The law forbade employers from interfering with employees as they exercised guaranteed rights, discharging or blacklisting employees for union activities or discriminating against employees who brought charges against a company. The full force of the federal government would back a union that was trying to bargain in good faith with an employer.

As might be expected business, which had done its best to defeat the legislation, criticized the law, especially the fact that it was so one-sidedly in favor of labor. It was freely forecast that the law would lead to great labor irresponsibility. Public opinion was squarely behind it, however, and people did not believe that labor would abuse its newly won privileges.

Although the Wagner Act was law, labor's struggle for recognition had not yet been won. One major obstacle still lay in the way. Only two weeks after President Roosevelt signed the Wagner Act into law, the American Liberty League issued a statement signed by fifty-eight lawyers who declared that the Wagner Act was unconstitutional. Earl F. Reed, counsel to the Wierton Steel Company and chairman of the Liberty League committee, stated that he would advise his clients not to feel bound by a law which he considered unconstitutional.

7

Labor on the March

THE C.I.O.

ATLANTIC CITY, NEW JERSEY, WAS HOST TO THE A.F. OF L.'S annual convention in October, 1935. William Green, the president who had taken over after Gompers' death, was presiding. Two of the delegates, John L. Lewis, president of the United Mine Workers, and William L. Hutcheson, president of the United Brotherhood of Carpenters and Joiners of America, were seated side by side.

A front-page article in *The New York Times* of October 20, 1935, told what hapened:

> Mr. Lewis moved over toward Mr. Hutcheson, and the two conversed in low tones. Delegates nearby said they heard Mr. Hutcheson call the miners' leader a foul name, whereupon Mr. Lewis, fully as broad as the carpenters' chief but not so tall, crashed his right fist into the taller man's jaw. Both went down fighting and they carried a table with them.
>
> While the delegates were in an uproar and President William Green pounded his gavel repeatedly for order, the heads

84

of the two largest and most powerful unions in the federation crashed to the floor pummeling at each other until separated by other delegates.

The fist fight marked the culmination of several defeats for the industrial unionists who were led by the miners' president.

For some time Lewis had felt that industrial unionism—like that of his United Mine Workers, which included all of the men working in the mines—rather than craft unions, like Mr. Hutcheson's carpenters, should be the goal of the A.F. of L. At the previous convention he had proposed that the A.F. of L. adopt industrial unionism, but a compromise had been agreed to and nothing was accomplished during the year. Accordingly, Lewis went to Atlantic City resolved to get action on his proposal. There were some who agreed with him, but the majority sided with Green, who looked askance at changing the traditional role of the A.F. of L., although he too had once advocated industrial unionism.

William Green's father, a Welsh coal miner, had come with his bride to Coshocton, Ohio, in 1870, and William, his first son, was born there on March 3, 1873. The family was extremely religious and young William hoped to study for the Baptist ministry, but his father could not afford to send him to a seminary. When fourteen the boy left school and worked as water boy on a railroad gang for fifty cents a week. At sixteen he became an apprentice in a coal mine.

He became interested in local union affairs, was elected secretary of the union at eighteen and later, its president. Next he was made president of the entire Ohio district and two years later resigned from the mine to spend full time on union business. In 1911 he was appointed statistician of the U.M.W. and was also elected to the Ohio Senate, where he worked hard for legislation that would improve working conditions. The workmen's compensation bill which he pushed through the legislature was used as a model by other states.

Green became secretary-treasurer of the U.M.W. in 1913 and also a member of the A.F. of L.'s executive council when John P. White, president of the U.M.W., refused the position as beneath his dignity. Green gradually worked his way up and by 1924 was third vice president, and late that year, thanks to the backing of his chief, John L. Lewis, was elected president. Among labor leaders Green stood out as a man of exceptional character. The father of five daughters and one son, he did not smoke, drink, swear or gamble, a rare combination in any profession!

Although Lewis resorted to oratory and threats, the majority of the delegates to that convention at Atlantic City clung to the Federation's traditional policy, thus forcing Lewis to take matters into his own hands. At the conclusion of the convention, with the encouragement of Sidney Hillman of the Clothing Workers, he invited those delegates who favored industrial unionism to meet with him and establish the Committee for Industrial Organization. It was not the group's intent to start a rival union but rather to undertake a program of education in order to advance collective bargaining in some of the mass-production industries.

Green declared that the group was rebelling against the wishes of the majority of the A.F. of L. in an effort to compel the Federation to accept their ideas. Lewis countered by submitting a one-sentence letter of resignation:

Dear Sir and Brother:

Effective this date I resign as a vice president of the American Federation of Labor.

Yours truly,
John L. Lewis

Immediately the C.I.O. started to plan its organizing campaign, but before proceeding out into the field, its leaders made peace overtures in January, 1936, and asked the A.F. of L. executive council for industrial charters in the automobile, radio, rubber and steel industries. Frightened by this rebellion, the council ordered the C.I.O. to disband, declaring that the organization was set up to advance the fortunes of "a few self-seeking individuals."

Outsiders were unimpressed at Lewis' break. The New York *Journal of Commerce* expressed the doubts of many when it declared:

Employers in mass-production industries do not minimize the changes in their industrial relations resulting from the entry of the new vertical union committee in the field. However, it is felt that improved wages and working conditions in these industries will militate against the success of the program.

Those who belittled the C.I.O. reckoned without Lewis and the others who joined the movement. New unions representing workers in automobiles, glass, radio, rubber and steel joined the organization, now called the Congress of Industrial Organizations, while leaders of the A.F. of L. begged them to return and threatened them if they did not. Eventually, in March, 1937, the C.I.O. unions were stricken from the membership of all city and state federations of the A.F. of L. Later that year the Federation made a last effort to woo the C.I.O. back, but Lewis preferred to keep his own union. Why should he return when he had enrolled 3,700,000 members compared with the A.F. of L.'s 3,400,000?

VICTORY IN STEEL

Philip Murray, the son of an Irish coal miner, was born in

Glasgow, Scotland, May 25, 1886. His mother died when he was two, thus forcing him to stay close to his father as he worked, and by ten Philip became a full-fledged miner too. Six years later, dissatisfied with working conditions, his father decided to immigrate to the United States where father and son settled near Pittsburgh and again entered the mines. Philip was an ambitious young man who took correspondence courses in economics and mathematics, enjoyed participating in athletics during his limited leisure time and was conscientious in practicing his Catholic religion.

Philip decided to dedicate his life to the union cause when he was only eighteen. One day after being cheated by a weighman he lost his patience and temper and the two fought. The young miner was fired, whereupon his 600 fellow miners went on strike, elected Philip president of their local and refused to work for a month. Hunger finally forced them to return to their jobs, and Murray was driven from the company town. A hard and able worker, he easily found another job but thereafter made affairs of the United Mine Workers his principal interest and advanced upward to become vice president of the union in 1920, the same year John L. Lewis was elected its president. During the 1920's when the coal industry suffered from depression and the U.M.W. was pulled and torn by Lewis' often arbitrary orders, Murray stuck by Lewis, although he differed with him politically. Murray, a stanch Democrat, supported Franklin D. Roosevelt for the presidency in 1932 but Lewis backed the Republican ticket of Herbert Hoover.

After the N.R.A. was adopted, members of the Amalgamated Association of Iron and Steel Workers urged their aged president, Michael Tighe, then in his mid-seventies, to take advantage of the new law. He refused, claiming that he had no funds to organize steelworkers and that it was impossible to overcome the anti-union position of the big steel companies. He recoiled when the rank and file suggested winning union recognition by a national strike, and after much dissension, an agreement was reached with John L. Lewis that provided for the Steel Workers Organizing Campaign, S.W.O.C., to be carried on with the help and under the direction of C.I.O. officials.

Murray was Lewis' natural choice to head the S.W.O.C. First he learned as much as he could about the industry, and then he hired 150 organizers and instructed them to go out, not hat in hand soliciting members, but offering to liberate the steelworkers. The promise of no initiation fees or union dues for a year helped win new members rapidly. When steel managements made adjustments or concessions to their employees, Murray would see that the S.W.O.C. took full credit, as it did when the United States Steel Corporation raised wages 10 per cent. He asserted that it was fear of S.W.O.C. that was responsible for the pay increase.

Again the corporations unleashed the usual anti-union propaganda, expanded their spy systems, fired outspoken unionists, intimidated their employees and accumulated stocks of munitions. Steelworkers signed up with the union nonetheless, and six months after the organizing had begun, S.W.O.C. boasted 125,000 members.

Barron's Weekly said this about S.W.O.C.: "For the first time in the history of the United States, industrial management is faced with a labor movement which is smart and courageous, wealthy and successful—a movement, moreover, which is winning its battle by applying a shrewd imitation of big business organization and technique."

It was now January of 1937. Sit-downers occupied two of

General Motors' Flint plants; the labor movement was becoming increasingly aggressive and militant; President Roosevelt's re-election had assured the continuance of the New Deal pro-labor government; the Wagner Act was being enforced to the best of the authorities' ability while waiting for the Supreme Court to decide its constitutionality; and the Senate's Civil Liberties Committee had listened to shocking testimony that told how business, in defiance of the law, had prevented employees from organizing or practicing collective bargaining. The comfortable days when big business was in the saddle and labor was kept in its place were gone. The social order was changing.

All these factors were carefully considered by Myron Taylor, chairman of the board of the United States Steel Corporation, and the bankers associated with the company. Further fighting with labor seemed futile to them, and they reasoned that it would be better to ensure continued steel production than risk a long strike. Taylor was told to settle with S.W.O.C. on the best possible terms. He and John L. Lewis met secretly in Washington on January 9, and after two months of meetings in New York and other cities, Benjamin Fairless, representing the corporation, and Philip Murray, representing the union, signed an agreement that permitted S.W.O.C. to represent its members, promised a forty-hour week, time and a half for overtime, a minimum of 62½¢ an hour, a week's vacation for those who had worked five years, a seniority system and machinery for settling grievances.

The news stunned both management and labor. Who would have dreamed that this powerful and traditionally anti-union corporation would make such an agreement without being forced by a strike? As for the workers, they rushed to join the S.W.O.C. locals, and membership grew to 400,000 by June.

More than one hundred smaller steel companies signed up with S.W.O.C., so that by May the only important holdouts were Bethlehem, Inland, Republic and Youngstown Sheet and Tube, known as the "Little Steel" companies. Tom Girdler, the forceful anti-union president of Republic, was their leader; and although 75,000 men walked out, he refused to recognize or bargain with the union. Instead, back-to-work movements were begun, picket lines were smashed, union headquarters were gassed, strike leaders arrested and strikebreakers imported and protected by militia.

Violence was inevitable. Three died in Massillon, two in Youngstown, one in Beaver Falls; others were crippled or injured. On May 30, at the Republic Steel Company's plant in South Chicago, some 1,500 strikers marched toward the plant, but they were stopped by 150 policemen.

Captain Thomas Kilroy ordered the crowd to disperse. A shower of bricks, rocks, steel bolts and other missiles was the strikers' answer. The police drew their revolvers, tear gas was released and then the police fired at the crowd. The unarmed strikers ran in every direction to escape, but seven were killed and scores were wounded. Union labor referred to the event as the "Memorial Day Massacre." A mass funeral was staged for the dead, and public sympathy was aroused, especially after it was proven that the strikers had not initiated the trouble.

Meanwhile, within the Republic plant the non-strikers (since they were afraid to pass through the picket lines) played Ping-pong and baseball during their off hours. Mayor Edwin Kelly of Chicago wrote the management of Republic that it was violating the city's housing and health ordinances by permitting the men to live in a factory not designed for residential use. He gave Republic forty-eight hours to vacate the men, and two days later twenty-one Pullman cars were shunted onto the property. These would house about 600 of the non-strikers, with the balance forced to take their chances coming and going each day.

"Little Steel" did not sign with the S.W.O.C., and the men eventually returned to work. Four years later each of the corporations was ordered by the National Labor Relations Board to recognize the United Steelworkers of America (the new name for S.W.O.C.), to rehire all employees who lost jobs because they belonged to the union or participated in strikes and to accept collective bargaining. By 1941 the C.I.O. affiliate had signed up 600,000 steelworkers, and union contracts had been negotiated in most of the industry.

The president of the new United Steelworkers of America was Philip Murray, the conservative, conscientious man who believed that the workers should give as well as take. He stood for no nonsense or dishonesty. "Never try to fool the men you represent," he instructed his staff. "Tell them what is possible and what it is impossible to do. And look upon a signed contract as something sacred—a pact to be observed; an agreement which is your bond of good faith."

A tribute to Murray's integrity was voiced by Myron Taylor in 1938:

"The union has scrupulously followed the terms of its agreement and, in so far as I know has made no unfair effort to bring other employees into its ranks, while the corporation subsidiaries, during a very difficult period, have been entirely free of labor disturbance of any kind."

THE U.A.W. AND GENERAL MOTORS

The United Automobile Workers was organized in August, 1935, when William Green appointed Francis J. Dillon president of the new union—despite protests of the delegates. By the following April the delegates voted to leave the A.F. of L., whereupon they elected Homer S. Martin their president and affiliated with the new C.I.O. John L. Lewis sent $100,000 and experienced organizers to begin signing up members in every automobile factory. A number of strikes called by the fledgling union were concluded successfully, thus giving the union prestige and strength. At last it was ready to tackle General Motors—but first it had to ferret out all company spies from the union.

Martin, the U.A.W. president, was a former Baptist minister who lost his Kansas City pulpit for being too sympathetic with the workingman's cause. (The feeling was that labor relations were no concern of the church.) He then worked for a Chevrolet plant but was fired because of his union work, whereupon he spent all his time helping the new U.A.W. He was a forceful and inspirational speaker, an ability which might have been largely responsible for his selection.

When Martin approached General Motors in December of 1936 and requested a conference to discuss working conditions, he was told that it was company policy for each plant to bargain with its own employees. Before the union officers had decided what to do next, the members decided for them by halting production on December 28 at the Cleveland Fisher Body plant, where they refused to work or leave their posts. The next day, when five union men requested collective bargaining and were fired from the Flint Fisher Body No. 2 plant, the men sat down at their machines. The larger Fisher Body plant was next to have its sit-downers after they discovered that the management was taking the dies out at night. By New Year's Day the men were firmly settled in the two Flint plants, and soon other General Motors plants were forced to close for lack of parts.

The corporation lost no time applying for an injunction which ordered the men to vacate the plants immediately. When union lawyers discovered that Judge Edward D. Black of Flint owned General Motors' stock worth almost $220,000, they had the injunction declared invalid, since a Michigan statute forbade judges from trying cases in which they had a personal interest. Because of this the company lost three weeks' time in the courts and reaped some unfavorable publicity while the sit-downers strengthened their positions.

The sit-down strike was a new technique in labor-management relations. It had been used a few times previously but never on such a large scale. There was no doubt that the men were morally and legally wrong in seizing private property and keeping the owners from using it. To their credit, however, it must be added that they protected the valuable dies and machinery, aired and cleaned the factories daily and maintained tight discipline within the plants. The basement cafeterias provided the only place to eat and smoke, the front and rear seats of half-assembled automobiles became beds and rubber floor mats the blankets. It was not easy for the men to keep warm after the management cut off all heat, but they made the best of things with daily chores to help pass the time.

The sudden sit-down in December had caught John L. Lewis by surprise. The C.I.O. was concentrating on organizing the steel industry, and he was not enthusiastic about being plunged into a conflict with General Motors and the thousands of bitter employees who were thrown out of work by the sit-down strikers. Nevertheless he pledged all support possible to the U.A.W. and its determination not to settle with General Motors until the corporation recognized it as the sole bargaining agent for all General Motors employees.

On January 4 Alfred P. Sloan, Jr., General Motors' president, declared, "General Motors will never recognize any union as the sole bargaining agency for all its employees."

Meanwhile George Boysen, a former General Motors employee and now the manager of a small factory, established the Flint Alliance with the hope of breaking the strike. With the backing of Flint's city manager, the police, anti-union citizens and executives of General Motors, he enrolled many General Motors workers in a back-to-work campaign. Union officials were called racketeers and communists, and Boysen urged that they be run out of town. All of this agitation finally brought violence on January 11 when police tried to block delivery of food to the sit-downers. The pickets who guarded the plant protested the interference; the sit-downers played fire hoses on the police; gunfire and tear gas followed with the pickets fighting back, but many were wounded before the police were routed in what later became known as the Battle of Bulls Run.

The following day Governor Frank Murphy, who had been elected with labor's help, dispatched the National Guard to Flint to keep the peace. He was in an extremely difficult position. He knew that the sit-down was illegal and that he must protect property rights, but he was sympathetic with the strikers' aims. Convinced that there would be terrible bloodshed if he ordered the soldiers to dislodge the men from the factories, he did his best to encourage the U.A.W. and General Motors to work out an amicable settlement.

Four days after the Battle of Bulls Run, the strikers and General Motors agreed on a peace truce by which the men would evacuate the plants and negotiations would then begin. However, that same day Boysen requested a conference to discuss collective bargaining as it would affect the "great majority of employees," whereupon the union called the peace deal off declaring that any agreement reached with Boysen would threaten their rights.

A few days later Lewis called upon President Roosevelt to do something to settle the strike. Labor had backed Roosevelt enthusiastically during his second campaign and at a rally before the election he had said: "Of course, we will continue every effort to end monopoly in business, to support collective bargaining."

In January Lewis told reporters:

> For six months last year the economic royalists such as Sloan, the duPonts, and other members of the General Motors family contributed their money and energy to drive the President—the administration—out of the White House. The administration asked labor to help repel this attack and labor helped. . . . The people of this country now expect the administration to do all it can in a legal way to repel this same rapacious enemy. . . . This is no time for pussyfooting, Labor is on the March!

President Roosevelt evaded the problem. "I think in the interest of peace there are moments when statements, conversation and headlines are not in order," he said.

The sit-downers remained intact, and the troops patrolled quietly until February 1, when a Women's Emergency Brigade consisting of about twenty women appeared, armed with clubs. It soon doubled in size and clashed with the police. A teen-age girl was said to have given orders to the police, a few windows were broken and then finally peace was restored. Two days later the court ordered the men out of the buildings and fined them $15,000,000.

"If the judge can get fifteen million bucks from us he's welcome to it, Buddy!"

96

"Tell the folks we can stay here till next Christmas," the sit-downers replied.

Governor Murphy still refused to order the troops into the factories and centered his efforts on settling the strike by negotiation. Finally, at noon on February 11, the forty-fourth day of the strike, Mr. Knudsen said as he signed the peace pact: "Let us have peace and make automobiles."

Under the terms of the agreement the union was recognized as the bargaining agency for its workers, the company agreed not to discriminate against union members, the union promised not to solicit members on company premises and to call off the sit-down strike. The company then had the injunction and fine canceled and topped it all off with a five cents an hour pay increase.

Flint had never seen such rejoicing! The sit-downers came out of the larger plant, two by two, clutching blankets, clothing and other articles they had used during the siege. All carried small American flags, and leading the procession was a color bearer proudly carrying a large American flag. A sound truck joined them blaring the song "Solidarity Forever," which was taken up by the marchers. The sit-downers were followed down the street by the Women's Emergency Brigade, its members wearing red and green berets and arm bands. The procession made its way past the thousands of people who lined Chevrolet Avenue and proceeded to the other plant, where the second group of sit-downers marched out triumphantly and joined the throng.

Although the union failed to win the closed shop which it had said it must have, the strike leaders hailed the pact as a notable advance. William Green called it a failure. Governor Murphy boasted that he would become the country's first Catholic president. General Motors suffered a costly work stoppage, and its anti-union policies were beaten for all time. John L. Lewis learned that President Roosevelt was not at his beck and call.

Other workers throughout the country decided that if the U.A.W. could do it in Flint so could they wherever there was trouble with stubborn employers. So sit-down strikes spread rapidly, affecting even the Woolworth stores, where clerks stood defiantly behind their counters refusing to wait on customers. However, the sit-down strategy was abandoned as public opinion and the courts both indicated their disapproval.

One obstacle still stood in the way of complete success for the U.A.W.—organizing the Ford Motor Company. Its elderly president, Henry Ford, was adamant that he would never recognize a union. His plant was honeycombed with spies under the direction of the ex-sailor pugilist Harry Bennett. Here the employees were so intimidated that they had little heart for joining any union.

In May, 1937, a group of C.I.O. union organizers approached an overpass to the Ford plant, preparing to pass out literature to employees. Ford's service men ordered them to leave, and in the ensuing scuffle one of the men, Walter Reuther, was savagely beaten in "The Battle of the Overpass." Later he testified:

"They picked me up about eight different times and threw me down on my back on the concrete. While I was on the ground they kicked me in the face, head, and other parts of my body. . . . I never raised a hand. After they kicked me down all the stairs then they started to hit me at the bottom of the stairs, hit me and slugged, driving me before them, but never letting me get away."

The U.A.W. reported to the National Labor Relations Board in 1938 those unfair practices of which it had proof from workers who were illegally fired or mistreated. By taking cases to courts and requesting numerous appeals and postponements, Ford delayed final decision and enforcement of the Wagner Act until 1941, when the Supreme Court upheld the findings of the Labor Board. Ford was ordered to rehire and pay $2,000,000 in back wages to the 2,566 workers who the Labor Board ruled had been discharged illegally for union membership.

A week later Ford bulletin boards displayed notices stating that employees were now free to organize if they so wished. Shortly thereafter Ford signed a contract with the U.A.W. which, in the union's own opinion, was "a model for the industry." Thus collective bargaining was won for the entire automobile industry.

THE C.I.O. AND POLITICS

During the hundred years that elapsed since the first workingmen's parties turned to politics in a vain effort to gain labor reforms, little was achieved by unions on the political front until 1936 when President Roosevelt ran for a second term. Labor leaders realized that if they hoped to keep a friend in the White House they would have to give him their active support. The A.F. of L. believed in strict non-partisanship but not so the C.I.O.! It affirmed its support of Roosevelt in 1936 by backing the formation of the Non-Partisan League and in New York State, the American Labor party. The C.I.O. contributed $500,000 to the Non-Partisan League which was non-partisan in name only, and at the same time Lewis declared that "labor has gained more under President Roosevelt than under any president in memory. Obviously it is the duty of labor to support Roosevelt 100 per cent in the next election."

"Join the C.I.O. and Help Build a Soviet America" was the title of one of the pamphlets published by anti–New Deal groups which sought to convince the public that the C.I.O. was radical, un-American and taking its directions from Moscow. It was true that there were some radicals in the C.I.O. and that the Communists hoped to seize control of the union or dominate it, but most of the leadership as well as the rank and file were loyal Americans.

Lewis, who backed Roosevelt's re-election, had been rebuffed when he suggested that the President intervene in the U.A.W. sit-down strike. Again, during the S.W.O.C. struggle with "Little Steel" Roosevelt impatiently declared "a plague on both your houses." Lewis smarted under these rebukes and became increasingly politically ambitious. According to one well-founded story Lewis proposed to Roosevelt that he run on the ticket as vice president in order to assure a third term victory, but nothing came of the suggestion—if indeed it had been made—and Lewis broke with Roosevelt and the New Deal in 1940. Always a controversial figure, Lewis previously had had some close association with the radical groups and was constantly feuding with other C.I.O. leaders. He declared in a carefully prepared speech on October 25, 1940, just before the election, that "the re-election of President Roosevelt for a third term would be a national evil of the first magnitude." His words went unheeded, however, and even his miners again voted for Roosevelt. At the next convention of the C.I.O. he retired as president, remaining, however, as head of the U.M.W.

Philip Murray became his successor but announced that he would not accept office unless the C.I.O. passed a resolution condemning communism. He was not going to let the C.I.O.

be a tool for Communists and other foreign subversive organizations. Although he opposed the United States becoming involved in the European War, he endorsed President Roosevelt's foreign policy and his national defense program.

8

The Shame of the Corporations

THE AMERICAN PUBLIC WAS ASTOUNDED TO LEARN THAT 282 corporations spent $9,440,132.15 on labor relations between January, 1933, and July, 1936—not to aid unemployed workers, improve their working conditions or raise their wages, but to demoralize labor unions, to destroy them through the use of strikebreakers and violence if necessary and to employ labor spies who watched their fellow employees, listened to their conversations and reported their activities to their employers. This was the way in which many large business firms sabotaged Section 7(a) of the National Labor Relations Act, which guaranteed workers the right to organize and bargain collectively.

These revelations came from the hearings which began in 1936 and were held by the Senate's Civil Liberties Committee, later to be better known as the La Follette Committee. The committee's subsequent report was based on its investigation of five of the nation's largest detective agencies—Burns, Corporations Auxiliary Company, National Corporation Service,

Pinkerton, and Railway Audit and Inspection—plus three major suppliers of tear and sickening gas, guns and ammunition—Federal Laboratories, Lake Erie Chemical Co., and Manville Manufacturing Co. The names of many other agencies were mentioned during the hearings as well as those of some 1,475 corporations which were listed as clients of such organizations. All told it was estimated that some 2,500 business firms contracted for spy services from about 200 agencies between 1933 and 1936, and in addition it developed that many companies maintained their own spies or obtained spy services from employers' associations. The committees described industrial sabotage as the most efficient method of preventing unions from forming, of wrecking them when they secured a foothold and of destroying them when they tried out their strength.

The spy fever spread as one agency spied on the other, one company on another and even the operatives of an agency on each other. Spying tends to feed on itself and breed new suspicions, so that soon various branches of the same corporation were building up their own "protective" systems. One professional spy told the committee: "In this business nobody trusts each other."

The Pinkerton agency, which enjoyed a gross business in 1935 of $2,300,000, had 1,000 regular employees and thousands of "contacts." Its principal industrial client had been General Motors until other well-known companies contracted for its services, firms like Bethlehem Steel, Pennsylvania Railroad, Radio Corporation of America, Baldwin Locomotive Works, B. F. Goodrich Company, Endicott-Johnson, Libby Owens Glass. The Chrysler Corporation was the chief client of Corporations Auxiliary Company, which also served General Motors, Campbell Soup, Quaker Oats, Timken Roller

Bearing Company, Fairbanks Morse, Royal Typewriter and many others.

As soon as the committee's investigators began their work, officials of detective agencies and certain corporations became apprehensive. When government agents arrived at the offices of some detective agencies with subpoenas requiring that their records be turned over to the committee, files were secretly destroyed and in some cases taken out the back door as the agents knocked at the front door.

In one instance, according to the committee's report:

> No sooner had subpoenas been served on the officers of the Railway Audit and Inspection Co., Inc., than they began a systematic and thorough destruction of the subpoenaed documents. Forewarned of this possibility, the committee subpoenaed the waste paper collected from the offices of this agency. From Pittsburgh, St. Louis, Atlanta, Philadelphia and New York, the committee began to receive bundles of torn fragments of paper which, upon reconstruction, proved to be journal sheets, card files of operatives, spy reports, letters from salesmen, and interoffice correspondence, all of which were documents specifically called for by the subpoena. To cap this flagrant course of misconduct, the officials of the agency refused to appear in person before the committee in response to the subpoena.

Industrial spying was justified by those who paid for it because it was, according to their spokesmen, "human engineering." This fancy term meant that it prevented sabotage and theft, it improved workers' efficiency, it improved relations between employees and employers and it protected industry against radicals and communists. Probing into the last reason, Senator Robert La Follette queried Mr. Littlejohn, the superintendent of Pinkerton's Atlanta branch:

SENATOR LA FOLLETTE: You have done a good deal of investigating, according to your ledger sheets, on radical and communistic activities, have you not, at your Atlanta office?

MR. LITTLEJOHN: Considerable.

SENATOR LA FOLLETTE: How many communists did you find?

MR. LITTLEJOHN: I don't believe we found any.

HOW THE LABOR SPY WORKED

According to the committee's report:

Every spy is assigned a code number or arbitrary initials which he uses instead of his real name. The code number is assigned to all correspondence between the spy and the agency. . . . A key to the code numbers is kept by the agency officials but apart from the record the name of the spy does not appear anywhere in the books. . . . Spy reports do not betray the identity of the spy because his name does not appear on them, only his symbol. The agency also tries to keep its name off the correspondence with a spy. For this reason the spy addresses his correspondence with the agency to a post-office box in the vicinity of the agency office. The box is rented under fictitious names . . . the spy is trained by the agency in little stratagems intended to avoid arousing the suspicion of his fellow employees . . . to . . . call from a pay station, to call collect, charges to be reversed to them, and never to call right after leaving work or right after a union meeting. Always go home and out of a back door and call.

"Red" Kuhl, a labor spy, explained to the committee how it was possible to "hook" a loyal union member.

"First you look your prospect over and if he is married that is preferable. If he is financially hard up, that is number

105

two. If his wife wants more money or he hasn't got a car, that all counts. And you go offer him this extra money; naturally you don't tell him what you want him for."

At first such a man would be asked to report union infractions of rules such as smoking or slovenliness. Next he is pressured for more damaging data, and because he fears exposure if he does not continue to tell, then—as the committee described his situation—he "slides further down the path of treachery that leads to deliberate espionage."

Many loyal union members found themselves trapped by these insidious labor spies. One minister inadvertently got himself "hooked" into a situation where he was forced to report on and betray members of his congregation.

J. H. Smith, another spy, described an operative as one who goes into a factory, joins the union and "gets all the information he possibly can concerning all dissatisfactions, discord, nepotism, anything at all that would tend to create an unpleasant feeling, and we give that information to our clients." Such an agent would usually be hired by the personnel department like any other employee, given a regular job on the assembly line or at a bench and placed on the factory payroll while also receiving a salary from the agency.

Apparently unions were honeycombed with industrial spies, and the records of one agency show the extent to which its detectives or spies had infiltrated unions. Some 304 of its employees were members, and of them 100 held offices from national vice president to local chairman.

Richard Frankensteen worked in the Dodge automobile plant, as did his father. Frankensteen was interested in organizing his fellow workers for the United Automobile Workers and became their chief organizer in his factory. As soon as he began his activities he became friendly with another worker,

John Andrews, also a Dodge employee. Andrews too wanted to see the union win recognition and was always urging a strike and violence. Again and again Frankensteen had to restrain his friend from provoking trouble, lest he wreck their plans.

The two men became so friendly that in 1935 during the usual summer layoff they rented a cottage at Lake Orion and vacationed there with their families. Andrews invited his rich uncle to join them, and Mr. Bath threw several parties for the adults while he lavished toys on the children.

Later, when Frankensteen sat in at the Senate hearing room, he heard Daniel G. Ross, sales manager for the Corporations Auxiliary, describe that vacation in the lakeside cottage. To his surprise and horror he learned that Andrews and his "uncle" were agents No. L-392 and FB assigned to spy on the leaders of the new union. For their services Chrysler had paid a bill of $1,152. In this way companies were able to "break" unions because they could discharge the ringleaders and members during the periods of seasonal layoffs. That a man might have a record of many years of loyal and good service made no difference.

Employees were not the only people corporations watched. During the strike of the Chevrolet workers at Toledo in 1935 a Pinkerton detective followed Edward F. McGrady, Assistant Secretary of Labor, who was acting as the federal conciliator in the case. R. L. Burnside, head of Pinkerton's office, told the committee that his instructions from Detroit were "to see who he was contacting, where he went."

STRIKEBREAKING

Strikebreakers were generally hired as guards "to protect personnel and property." Their duties often called for provoking violence so that the police would be goaded into arresting the union leaders and public opinion would be turned against the strikers. The Ford Motor Company, whose president opposed unionization and believed that the National Labor Relations Board was unconstitutional, had its own protective force, the Ford Service Organization, under the command of a former prizefighter. It became notorious for its brutal methods of handling strikes.

Many of the strikebreakers had criminal records or came from the underworld. In 1932, seven of the thirteen strikebreakers Railway Audit and Inspection Company had put into a St. Louis strike were wanted by police of other cities for various serious charges. The following year some seven hundred guards, recruited mostly in Chicago and New York, were brought to the Milwaukee plant of the Wisconsin Light and Power Company. An employee of the Railway Audit and Inspection Company testified that "about 20 per cent" had police records.

Strikebreakers and company guards were ineffective without arms, and these were readily available from several suppliers. One of them, Lake Erie Chemical Company, enjoyed more than twice as much business in 1934 as in 1932 as it sold gas and gas equipment to many large corporations. Many of the shipments were sent to dummy accounts in order to hide the purchasers' identities.

In 1933 Lake Erie's Detroit salesman wrote the factory asking that a shipment of guns, clubs and shells be sent to the police chief at Flint, Michigan. "Do not bill the City of Flint for this material," the letter said. "Instead bill to the Manufacturers' Association of Flint, 901 Industrial Bank Building. For your information only, I have reason to believe this material is for the Chevrolet Motor Co."

In correspondence advertising its products, the Manville Company had this to say about the effectiveness of its wares:

> Our equipment was used to break up the strike of the Ohio Rubber Co., at Willoughby, Ohio, and to break up the strike of the gear plant at Toledo, Ohio; was used at the Eaton Axle plant at Cleveland; at the Real Silk Hosiery Co. at Indianapolis; and at a great many small places. In each of the above cases, the equipment was used by the detective agencies brought in.

In its conclusions the La Follette Committee stated: "The public cannot afford to let this challenge presented by industrial espionage go unnoticed. Through it private corporations dominate their employees, deny them their constitutional rights, promote disorder and disharmony, and even set at naught the powers of the government itself."

JUSTICE AT LAST

Once the committee hearings had revealed the true story of what the corporations had done to obstruct the law and prevent the formation of unions, public opinion swung sharply away from business and toward labor. Newspapers criticized industry for denying labor its civil liberties. Many people denounced those corporations that had been guilty of such practices, and most stopped these objectionable activities. The public was aroused, however, and demanded that labor receive protection.

About this same time the Supreme Court started to hear a number of cases involving the constitutionality of the Wagner Act. President Roosevelt asked Congress for authority to reorganize the courts, which had invalidated numerous New Deal laws. While congressmen were angrily debating the President's request, the Supreme Court handed down its decision upholding Congress' authority to regulate labor conditions as it had done in the Wagner Act.

In the five to four decisions in *N.L.R.B. v. Jones and Laughlin,* Chief Justice Hughes said:

> Employees have as clear a right to organize and select their representatives for lawful purposes, as the respondent has to organize its business and select its own officers and agents. Discrimination and coercion to prevent the free exercise of the right of employees to self-organization and representation is a proper subject for condemnation by competent legislative authority.

Immediately the N.L.R.B. went to work handling thousands of cases, settling strikes and conducting elections. Within the next eight years it had handled 36,000 unfair labor practice cases and 38,000 employee representation cases. In addition it conducted 24,000 elections in which some 6,000,000 workers were involved.

Out went company unions, "yellow dog" contracts, blacklists, labor spies, anti-union propaganda. Approximately 300,000 employees regained their jobs and $9,000,000 back pay. The closed shop and peaceful picketing would hereafter be taken as much for granted as the right to vote. After more than a hundred years of struggle, labor was free to organize and bargain collectively, and its rights were secured by the highest court of the land.

9

Labor and World War II

TEN DAYS AFTER THE JAPANESE ATTACKED PEARL HARBOR on December 7, 1941, President Roosevelt summoned business and labor leaders to a conference in Washington. He was anxious to avoid passage of an anti-union law which Congress was considering. He felt that business and labor could take advantage of the strong spirit of national unity that had swept over the country and work out an agreement that would keep strikes to a minimum during the war. As Wake Island and Hong Kong fell to the Japanese, the group finally agreed on three main points: all labor differences would be settled peacefully, lockouts and strikes would be banned during the war period and a labor board would be established to settle all disputes. The question of union security during the war was left unsolved, but President Roosevelt ruled that the new War Labor Board should settle that problem.

The following month an executive order provided that the War Labor Board (W.L.B.) consist of twelve members, equally divided among business, labor and the public. Once the Secretary of Labor had certified that a labor-management dispute "might interrupt work which contributes to the effective prosecution of the war," the W.L.B. would take the case and its decision would be binding. In addition the W.L.B. was given authority to control both hours of work and wages. One of the board's first acts was to decide the union security problem by devising the so-called maintenance of shop agreement. Although neither closed nor open shops could be enforced, for the duration of hostilities unions were protected because members were required to maintain their memberships during the life of their union contract, and if they refused to do so they were to be discharged.

LITTLE STEEL FORMULA

Strikes immediately declined as labor maintained a fine record of almost uninterrupted production, but another problem arose to plague the W.L.B.—the matter of wage increases.

Spiraling prices pushed up the cost of living and naturally led to a demand for higher wages. At first the W.L.B. considered each request for a wage increase on its own merit and granted it when justified. There were definite signs of runaway inflation, however, unless something was done to control prices and wages, and the W.L.B. sought some over-all program that would stabilize the cost of goods and labor.

In July, while German submarines were sinking one of every four Allied ships and the Japanese were conquering most of the Far East, the employees of the Little Steel companies demanded an increase of a dollar a day. Hearings were held, and it was finally agreed by members of the W.L.B. that wage advances would be granted in amounts no greater than the cost of living increase that occurred between January, 1941, and May, 1942. Data prepared by the Bureau of Labor Statistics

Children working in a cotton mill in the early 1900's.

Family working at home making artificial flowers, 1908.

Photo by Lewis W. H

Sweatshop, New York City, 1912.

Scene of the Haymarket riot, May 4, 1886.

Fight between strikers and the Pinkertons at Homestead, Pennsylvania, July 5, 1892.

sing the Blue Eagle of the
A over Rockefeller Center,
v York City, September 11,
3.

Members of the Labor Advisory Committee meet with Hugh S. Johnson, administrator the NRA, 1933. At Johnson's right is Frances Perkins, Secretary of Labor.

General Motors strike at Flint, Michigan, February 4, 1937.

attle of the Overpass between Ford servicemen and members of the United Automobile Workers. Third from right is Walter Reuther.

Valter Reuther gives packages of leaflets to members of UAW-CIO women's auxiliary for distribution at Ford plant, May 26, 1937.

UAW mass meeting in Cadillac Square, March 23, 1937.

Workers leaving plant after striking at Dodge Motor Car Co.

Terence Powderly, President of the Knights of Labor.

Eugene V. Debs, noted Socialist and labor leader.

Samuel Gompers, Foun
of the American Federa
of Labor.

Sidney Hillman, first President of the Amalgamated Clothing Workers.

David Dubinsky, President of the International Ladies' Garment Workers Union.

Photo by Harry Rubenstein

n L. Lewis, former Pres-
nt of the United Mine
rkers.

Chase Ltd. Photo

William Green, former President of the American Federation Labor.

George Meany, President of the AFL-CIO.

Philip Murray, former President of the Congress of Industrial Organizations.

es R. Hoffa, President of International Brotherhood eamsters, Chauffeurs, Ware-semen and Helpers.

Chase Ltd. Photo

Blue Ribbon Board representing government and industry makes plans for taking census of unemployed, 1937.

Representatives of Labor, Management and Government meet in Washington at outbreak of World War II to work out agreement to end work stoppages in defense industries

Merger of AFL-CIO, December 5, 1955.

Interior of a Diesel cab showing fireman seated at left. Railroads contend that this extra crew member is unnecessary (featherbedding).

Members of the Teamsters' Union loading a truck.

Assembly line at American Motors Corp.

Members of the UAW working at a Chrysler plant.

Photo by Sam Reiss

Bank owned and operated by Amalgamated Clothing Workers.

Unity House, vacation resort founded and operated by ILGWU.

Machine capable of milling, drilling, boring, tapping and reaming automatically from instructions expressed numerically on punched tape. (automation)

showed this to be 15 per cent, and it was this amount that was then granted Little Steel workers who, when the 15 per cent was applied, received forty-four cents a day in additional wages instead of a dollar. This formula resulting in 15 per cent increases became known as the Little Steel formula.

With the passage of the Economic Stabilization Act in October of 1942, the W.L.B. was required to limit all subsequent wage increases to 15 per cent except when unusual conditions prevailed. Labor supported the Little Steel formula, but as prices continued to rise it grew restive, since the farmers and industrialists were making money while wage earners suffered a decline in the purchasing power of their money. Nevertheless, unions abided by the Little Steel formula, for they recognized that it was the only means of keeping prices in check and preventing inflation.

One labor leader who was determined to share in the temporary wartime prosperity was John L. Lewis. The previous October he had taken the U.M.W. out of the A.F. of L. after a dispute with Philip Murray. Long before the U.M.W.'s contract was due to expire on April 30, 1943, he announced that his 530,000 men would take nothing less than a two dollars a day increase including portal to portal pay for time spent traveling underground to and from work. As for the W.L.B. —Lewis did not recognize its authority. Although he had no intention of calling a strike of the miners while the nation was at war, he did take great care to point out that without a contract his miners would never "trespass on the property of the coal operators."

THE NON-TRESPASSING MINERS

As April 30 approached there was a rash of strikes, slow-downs and stoppages above ground. In Johnstown, Pennsyl-

113

vania, a strike of bus and streetcar operators stranded workers and other citizens. In Lima, Ohio, 4,000 employees struck a plant because the company failed to dismiss a few workers who were not putting 10 per cent of their wages into war bonds. Some 2,000 Chrysler workers in Detroit were idled by 500 men who walked out in a wildcat strike when a man was suspended for "smoking and loitering." John L. Lewis' own District 50, the catchall union he had established for unorganized workers who did not fit into existing organizations, was on strike for two weeks at a plant of the Celanese Corporation of America. When President Roosevelt told the union men to return to work they obeyed promptly. Other members of Lewis' U.M.W. union were not so docile, however.

Before the April 30 deadline many of the miners failed to show up at the tipples. With industry working around the clock, huge quantities of coal were needed, and there was only enough soft coal above ground to last for forty-three days. On May 1 Secretary of the Interior Harold L. Ickes told the 4,000 coal operators to hoist the American flag above the mine shafts and display the posters "United States Government Property," which he was mailing to them. He also promised to send troops to maintain order if necessary.

The following day President Roosevelt ordered the mines seized and that evening prepared to go on the radio to order the miners back to work. The beetled-browed miners' leader scooped him, however, by announcing just twenty-two minutes before the President was scheduled to speak that a fifteen-day truce had been reached. This allowed time for him to work out the contract with Secretary Ickes.

"Tomorrow the Stars and Stripes will fly over the coal mines. I hope every miner will be at work under that flag," the President said in the course of his anticlimactic speech. The miners

114

did go back to work for their new employer, the United States government, and the truce was later extended to the end of May when a new crisis developed because no agreement had been reached. Again the miners laid down their tools.

Forty-eight hours later President Roosevelt once more took to the radio to declare: "As President and Commander-in-Chief, I order and direct the miners . . . to return to their work on Monday, June 7, 1943." The men did not return because the President of the United States had ordered them to their jobs but because Lewis told them to resume work "up to and including June 20 only."

By this time the public and Congress were furious at the miners. Protests were raised by men in the armed forces who felt that the miners had no right to strike and should be drafted if they chose to remain away from work. Lewis was pictured as a man who had betrayed his country. The A.F. of L. and C.I.O. recognized that Lewis was fighting for all labor in protesting that the Little Steel formula was inadequate and therefore unfair to labor. Nevertheless, the C.I.O. denounced him as a troublemaker, but the A.F. of L. held its peace and later readmitted the U.M.W. after the dispute was settled.

Twice again there were work stoppages as the W.L.B. refused to approve agreements that violated the Little Steel formula. At last, in October, a complicated formula was worked out which gave the miners an increase of $1.50 a day, portal to portal and vacation pay, all within the Little Steel formula and therefore with the blessing of the W.L.B.

THE SMITH-CONNALLY ACT

As had often happened, Lewis had again won a victory for his miners but hurt labor as a whole. In the midst of the dispute

115

between the miners and the government, Congress adopted the Smith-Connally Act, which President Roosevelt vetoed because he thought it would make labor more restive and it ran counter to labor's no-strike pledge. Congress quickly enacted the bill over the veto, reflecting the public's disapproval of irresponsible labor leaders like Lewis.

The new law provided (1) that strikes could not be called until a vote had been conducted by the N.L.R.B. during a thirty-day cooling-off period; (2) that the government could seize any plant if workers stopped production and thus threatened the war effort; (3) that anyone who started or promoted a strike in a seized plant might be subject to criminal penalties; and (4) that unions could not contribute to political campaign funds.

The Smith-Connally Act did not hurt the labor cause as President Roosevelt had feared. After the railroad unions threatened a strike if they did not obtain a higher wage increase than permitted by the Little Steel formula, the W.L.B. devised a means of helping labor receive added income by authorizing fringe benefits—premium pay for night work, bonuses, incentive pay, additional holidays and vacation days with pay, greater allowances for lunch or travel time, health, insurance and pension plans. This had the effect of voiding the Little Steel formula, which displeased management but satisfied labor sufficiently to lower the number of strikes to a third of the prewar average. After Congress passed the Smith-Connally Act, labor-management relations improved greatly, for there were only fifty labor disputes in which the N.L.R.B. recommended that the President seize the plants. Twenty-three were because employers refused to obey decisions, twenty-six because unions defied decisions and one because neither labor nor management could reach a decision.

CLEAR IT WITH SIDNEY

After many pro-labor and liberal congressmen were defeated in the 1942 fall elections and the Smith-Connally Act had been passed, the C.I.O. leaders realized that something would have to be done to improve labor's position. It was evident that President Roosevelt must be re-elected in 1944 and with him a Congress that would be favorable to labor. To accomplish this goal the Political Action Committee (P.A.C.) was created with Sidney Hillman its chairman and R. J. Thomas the treasurer.

Sidney Hillman, a small man with a shock of black, wiry hair and a big nose, was born in Zagare, Lithuania, in 1887 of Jewish parents. His father, a wool merchant, sent the boy to the little town's Talmudic seminary when he was twelve. Here Sidney became interested in the sciences and at fifteen left school to become a laboratory assistant in a chemical plant.

He joined the Lithuanian underground trade union movement during the revolution of 1905 and two years later, when he was twenty, came to Chicago, where he signed up as an apprentice cutter in the clothing factory of Hart, Schaffner and Marx. He earned only seven dollars a week for a tiring twelve-hour day, but when he had finished work each evening he hurried to Hull House to study English and economics.

Men of many nationalities worked in the shop, most of them earning two to four dollars a week for sixty to eighty-four hours work. Hillman's fellow workers, who soon thought of him as an authority on labor matters, looked to him for leadership although he was then only twenty-three. In 1910 he compiled a list of grievances and organized a strike of pressers, tailors, trimmers and spongers in the plant. Hillman did his best to unite them, but the ethnic groups mistrusted each other and the strike failed. During January of the following year the

117

rank and file asked him to represent them at Hart, Schaffner and Marx to set up a procedure for settling grievances. He was elected president of the newly organized Amalgamated Clothing Workers three years later and remained at its head until his death in 1946.

Hillman believed that the union had a responsibility to assist the clothing manufacturer. "We help the employer for one excellent reason," he declared in 1923. "The clothing workers must make their living out of the clothing industry—just like their employers." The Amalgamated worked closely with employers, cooperating in such ways as lending them money when necessary and performing valuable and costly research for them. Because of this unusual approach to union responsibility, Hillman and Franklin D. Roosevelt became close friends.

John L. Lewis and Hillman were instrumental in forming the C.I.O. and thereafter Hillman kept a close watch on the union's progress. He was also responsible for forming the Textile Workers Organizing Committee, which won 400,000 members in 1937, three years after the United Textile Workers had suffered a serious defeat in 1934. By the time the United States entered World War II, Hillman was a nationally known figure in union circles.

The Dies Committee on Un-American Activities investigated the P.A.C. and stated that it was "a subversive Communist campaign to subvert the Congress of the United States to its totalitarian program." Others attacked the P.A.C. as a radical un-American group run by Communists who were supporting Roosevelt's re-election. Even Hillman was slandered and called a Communist because he was a Jew and foreign-born, but a subsequent investigation by the F.B.I. left no doubts of his loyalty to America.

Under Hillman's aggressive and imaginative leadership,

P.A.C. literature flooded the country telling labor chiefs and leaders of the Democratic party how to plan and run political campaigns effectively. At the Democratic convention of 1944 President Roosevelt instructed his manager that party platform planks and all important strategy must be "cleared" with Hillman. "Clear it with Sidney" became the immediate slogan of his Republican opponents who charged Hillman with being a Communist as well as a labor leader who had great power in the Roosevelt administration. Little wonder the Republicans were horrified at the activities of this union political machine which Hillman had created.

The House Committee on Un-American Activities charged that P.A.C. was a "subversive Communist organization." Governor John Bricker of Ohio said the P.A.C. was "trying to dominate our government with radical and communistic schemes." All of labor's foes and the anti-Roosevelt forces did what they could to attack the organization. Nevertheless, Roosevelt won a fourth term, and there were many governors, senators and representatives whom P.A.C. claimed it helped elect. The P.A.C. had reached its zenith, however, and with Hillman's withdrawal it gradually faded out.

By the close of the war, labor had strengthened its position. There were 14,000,000 members in the A.F. of L. and the C.I.O. The War Labor Board had protected unions and enabled them to prosper. And through the award of fringe benefits major innovations were established in collective bargaining which would greatly improve labor's welfare during the years to come.

10 ⊂⊑

Diary of a Strike

WHEN WORLD WAR II ENDED WITH THE FALL OF JAPAN ON August 14, 1945, there was great cause for joy, though few people realized that victory brought with it not only peace but tremendous problems of reconverting our industrial war machine back to peacetime production.

Even before V-J Day many companies were cutting back operations as they canceled overtime and reduced wages to prewar rates. Now that the war was over, most of the 12,000,-000 men and women in the armed forces would be back shortly in the labor force. Some 100,000 contracts worth $20,-000,000,000 were canceled by the Navy and War Departments, and unemployment soon rose to over 3,000,000. Many factories closed in order to retool for civilian production, while some shut their doors permanently. A return to the forty-hour week brought a drastic reduction in take-home pay, while rising prices threatened an inflationary spiral. Little wonder that there was grumbling as workingmen worried about job security and urged that hourly rates be increased in order to keep their former wartime purchasing levels.

In June of 1945 Walter Reuther, vice president of the United Automobile Workers, published a pamphlet, "The Challenge of Peace." This asserted his belief that industry could pay higher wages out of its profits, and not by raising prices, because that often canceled the benefit of pay increases. On August 16 President Truman signed Executive Order No. 9599, which decreed that wages might be raised only if they were not followed by price increases. Two days later Reuther asked the General Motors management to reopen its contract, since it contained a clause which provided that wage provisions might be reopened by either party in event of a change in the national wage policy.

In line with the President's order, Reuther requested a 30 per cent increase in pay and insisted that it could be granted without raising the price of cars. Similar demands were made on Ford and Chrysler, but it was apparent that the showdown would come between General Motors and the U.A.W. It was Reuther's idea to strike the automobile manufacturers "one at a time," since this would hurt General Motors more than a general industry strike.

A NEW KIND OF LABOR LEADER

Walter, the smallest of the four Reuther brothers, was born in Wheeling, West Virginia, on September 1, 1907. Valentine Reuther, a German immigrant who believed in socialism, raised Walter and his three brothers to value freedom and justice and taught them how to express themselves clearly on all subjects. The boys learned to speak convincingly and think quickly as they participated in the family's Sunday afternoon debates on topics like the right to strike or capital punishment.

121

At sixteen Walter left Wheeling High School to help support the family and became a toolmaker's apprentice at Wheeling Steel. He was discharged three years later when he tried to organize the men in a protest against work on Sunday. Since Detroit seemed to offer greater opportunity, he went there and found a job at Briggs Motors, where he worked a thirteen-hour night shift, then switched to Ford, where as a skilled toolmaker he earned $1.10 an hour. Roy and Victor, his brothers, soon joined him.

Walter had always been an ambitious boy, eager to get ahead and willing to work hard for advancement. While at Ford he worked nights, attended classes during the daytime and, when he had finished high school, continued his studies at Wayne University, where he concentrated for the next three years on the social sciences. Here he was active in the radical student movement, involved himself in the Socialist party and in 1932 campaigned actively for Norman Thomas, the Socialist presidential candidate.

His greatest interest lay in the union movement, for he felt that unionism was absolutely necessary for the then unorganized automobile workers. This conviction cost him his foreman's job at Ford in 1933. Unable to find work because of the depression, he took his savings and invited Victor to join him in a trip to Germany. From there the brothers traveled to Russia, where Walter trained young men in toolmaking; then the pair continued their journey to the Far East and eventually returned to Detroit in 1935. The following year he married auburn-haired Mae Wolf, a physical education instructor whom he had known for some time. On their wedding night the couple drove out of town to attend a meeting where Reuther made a speech. Nothing interfered with his union work!

Walter joined the General Motors Ternstedt plant and devoted all his free time to union activities, becoming president of a new union, whereupon he was fired and blacklisted. He decided to apply all his time and energy to organizing and strengthening the local, which had only seventy-eight members. With the help of Victor and other men who worked at the Kelsey Hayes Wheel factory, he planned a sudden sit-down strike which caught the unsuspecting management off guard. In return for calling off the strike, Reuther was allowed to sign up other members, and Local 174 soon expanded to 30,000 members!

The Reuther brothers were active in the General Motors sit-down strike of 1937, and Walter soon became a leader of the U.A.W. as well as the unionist in charge of the General Motors division. His fame spread rapidly when he, Richard Frankensteen and other U.A.W. leaders were beaten by Ford servicemen in the 1937 "Battle of the Overpass." In 1938 thugs broke into Reuther's home and again thrashed him unmercifully.

Reuther built an image of himself quite unlike that of the average labor leader. The idea of winning a few cents an hour wage increase did not strike him as the real role of a union chief. Instead he brought imagination to the job, built a powerful union, made the name of Walter Reuther stand for aggressive leadership and demonstrated ability to deal successfully with his union members and at the same time develop prestige in the public eye.

Neither a drinker nor a smoker, he always dressed well and had the appearance of a fastidious businessman rather than a labor leader. Called a "pseudo-intellectual nitwit" by John L. Lewis, Reuther's intelligence could not be denied, nor could his iron nerve and fierce loyalty to the union cause. It was this fanatical devotion to the labor movement that prompted Reu-

123

ther to make his demand in 1945, that General Motors grant the union a 30 per cent increase without raising the prices of its cars. He argued that the size of the corporation's profits made this possible and that the increase would help sustain general purchasing power.

It happened that this request was to trigger more than a routine labor dispute between the U.A.W. and General Motors. It made the pattern for other settlements and represented a new kind of ideological battle. Instead of haggling over pennies, Reuther insisted that the company pay higher wages without passing the added cost on to the consumer. Nevertheless, although he believed that a company should grant the maximum increase possible without having to raise prices, he was willing to discuss and bargain the matter with each company and adjust his demands in accordance with the concern's ability to pay.

The negotiations which followed the reopening of the contract between General Motors and the U.A.W. were unusual and have provided an interesting picture of what happens when management of a large corporation and leaders of a major labor union square off against each other. For the sake of brevity last names only appear in the following text. They are identified below:

Anderson—Harry W. Anderson, vice president of labor relations, General Motors.

Coen—Harry Coen, assistant director of personnel, General Motors.

Garrison—Lloyd W. Garrison of the University of Washington, chairman of the special fact-finding board.

Merritt—Walter G. Merritt, attorney for General Motors.

Reuther—Walter Reuther, vice president of the U.A.W.

Schwellenbach—Louis B. Schwellenbach, Secretary of Labor.

Thomas—Roland J. Thomas, president of the U.A.W.
Truman—Harry Truman, President of the United States.
Wallace—Henry Wallace, Secretary of Commerce.
Wilson—Charles E. Wilson, president of General Motors.

DIARY OF A STRIKE

October, 1945

The company rejected the 30 per cent increase because it would not give "fifty-two hours' pay for forty hours' work." Reuther then announced that the union would take less than 30 per cent if the company could prove that it was unable to make a fair profit. Negotiations commenced between the company and the union while Wilson first conferred with Truman, then offered a new plan for a forty-five to forty-eight hour workweek with a 5–8 per cent basic hourly wage increase over three to five years. Reuther quickly turned down this offer, the union took a strike vote and negotiations were suspended.

An excerpt from the transcript of the negotiations gives some insight into what goes on when labor and management carry on collective bargaining sessions.

COEN: Is the U.A.W. fighting for the whole world?

REUTHER: We have been fighting to hold prices and increase purchasing power. We are making our little contribution in that respect.

COEN: Why don't you get down to your size and get down to the type of job you are supposed to be doing as a trade union leader and talk about the money you would like to have for your people and let the labor statesmanship go to hell for a while?

REUTHER: Translate that so I know what you mean. . . .

I understand you think our position makes it more difficult to work out a solution because we are getting into issues that lie outside the narrow limits of collective bargaining. Instead of talking about wages, what we want, and sticking to that, we are talking about prices and profits.

COEN: That is very well stated. Nobody else is doing that but you. You are the fellow that wants to get the publicity out of this whole thing. You want to enhance your own political position. That is what the whole show is about.

REUTHER: I see.

COEN: Do you believe we have to learn to live 50 per cent better, or do you believe first we have to learn how to create that much more wealth? What does that have to do with dividing up profits and reducing the salaries of the people in the corporation?

REUTHER: Because unless we get a more realistic distribution of America's wealth, we won't get enough to keep this machine going.

COEN: There it is again. You can't talk about this thing without expressing your socialistic desires.

REUTHER: If fighting for a more equal and equitable distribution of the wealth of this country is socialistic, I stand guilty of being a socialist.

November, 1945

Wallace made public a report of the Commerce Department that showed industry could raise wages 15 per cent in 1946 and another 10 per cent in 1947 without increasing prices. Reuther then asked that a federal conciliator be assigned to the negotiations when resumed but the company refused to admit a conciliator until collective bargaining had failed. The company thereupon offered a new living cost rise equal to an 8–10 per cent wage increase but Reuther rejected the proposal. The company then suggested a wage increase of 10 per cent and a forty-five hour workweek for all hourly workers. To this Reuther said "no" and called his members out on strike.

Although Truman announced that he would pursue a hands-off policy, Schwellenbach said that he would invite the company and the union to Washington to arbitrate. The company refused to consider this proposal until the union had modified its demands and dropped the profits and price issue.

While negotiations were being conducted the company published a series of advertisements in which it stated that the "open the books" demand of the U.A.W. was "interference with prerogatives of management." The company asked pointed questions such as, "Is the Union Seeking Facts or New Economic Power?" "A Look at the Books, or a Finger in the Pie?" From its pamphlet: "Here Is the Issue," the company said:

> A "look at the books" is a clever catch phrase intended as an opening wedge whereby unions hope to pry their way into the whole field of management.
>
> The fact is that the U.A.W.-C.I.O. is reaching for power. . . .
>
> It leads surely towards the day when union bosses, under the threat of strike, will seek to tell us what we can make, when we can make it, where we can make it, and how much we can charge. . . .

December, 1945

Truman told the G.M. employees to end their strike and the company to get back into production, calling the strike a "major obstacle holding up our reconversion program." The company and the union thereupon resumed negotiations, but the meetings deadlocked because the company refused to budge from its 10 per cent offer. Truman thereupon appointed a fact-finding board under Garrison which the company ignored as it again stated that any agreement reached must continue the open shop.

Truman insisted that the fact-finding board be permitted to examine the company's books, since the wage dispute centered about its ability to pay. The fact-finding board took no action, however, hoping that the company and the union would resume collective bargaining, which they did as they signed an agreement to the effect that they would settle the dispute by themselves.

When Truman announced that the "ability to pay" issue was a legitimate matter for his fact-finding board to investigate, Merritt withdrew from the fact-finding hearing. He stated that the company did not plead inability to pay as a reason for rejecting any wage consideration, but that the "ability to pay" issue was a threat to free enterprise and the industry. Garrison said that he would continue the inquiry just the same.

January, 1946

In January of 1946 more than 1,650,000 industrial workers were idled as electrical, packing house, steel and other industries were shut by strikes. Washington was pressured to permit price increases and repudiate the stand taken by the fact-finding board, which issued a report stating that G.M. could give a 19½ cents hourly wage increase without raising prices. Finally the Truman administration said that it would permit an increase in steel prices after the companies had come to terms with the C.I.O. Soon many unions signed for 18½ cents an hour, and nothing was said about increasing prices.

Throughout all of this, however, the G.M. strike and negotiations dragged on as the company rejected the recommendation of the fact-finding board. Still offering 10 per cent, it said that an agreement must come from collective bargaining, not a government ruling. Two and half weeks later the company modified its stand by saying that it would not change its wage offer until other contract provisions had been agreed upon.

February, 1946

On February 12 the United Electrical Workers, C.I.O., signed a contract with G.M. for its 30,000 workers, providing for a wage increase of 19 cents an hour, one-half cent below the recommendation of the President's fact-finding committee. The U.A.W. called it a "double cross," and its leaders were especially angered because the head of the United Electrical Workers had not told Reuther that he was negotiating with G.M. Having settled with the electrical workers for 18 cents the company offered the same to the U.A.W. Reuther immediately denounced the offer, whereupon Wilson and Thomas held a series of talks but without any results. On the last day of the month at a bedside conference Wilson gave the final terms before he left for the hospital.

March, 1946

The union rejected Wilson's final offer, and Anderson took Wilson's place as negotiations again resumed. Several days later the U.A.W. accepted the 18½ cents hourly increase and the 113-day strike ended.

The right of a union to look at a company's books did not become an issue again between General Motors and the U.A.W., although it kept coming up again and again in other labor disputes. In 1956 the Supreme Court ruled in *N.L.R.B. v. Truitt Manufacturing Company* that a union could look at the company's books in a case where an employer mechani-cally repeats a claim of inability to pay, without making the slightest effort to substantiate the claim. The court stated: "We do not hold, however, that in every case in which eco-nomic inability is raised as an argument against increased wages it automatically follows that the employees are en-titled to substantiating evidence. Each case must turn upon its facts."

Relations between the U.A.W. and General Motors im-proved greatly after 1946 and produced in 1950 an unusual and precedent-setting collective-bargaining agreement. This provided for special insurance benefits, a pension, cost-of-living adjustments based on price changes reported by the Bureau of Labor Statistics and an annual "improvement fac-tor"—a 2.5 per cent pay rise to let workers share in increased productivity due to better machines. In 1955 Reuther fol-lowed up with his famous "guaranteed annual wage," which provides that unemployed workers receive 60 to 65 per cent of their normal earnings over a six-month period, the company paying the difference between unemployment compensation and the guaranteed wage. All of these benefits were won by the union from each of the major automobile manufacturers without costly strikes and violence.

What a change had taken place in the automobile industry since the early 1930's when workers were fired for joining a union or participating in union activities!

11 ☞

Postwar Adjustments

JOHN L. LEWIS AGAIN!

The General Motors workers had scarcely gone back to work before John L. Lewis announced new demands for the miners that included a wage increase, the financing of health and welfare services, better safety practices and the right to shut any mine they considered unsafe. April 1, 1946, was the deadline, but the operators refused to sign a contract that included health and welfare insurance because they thought that this had nothing to do with collective bargaining over wages and hours of work.

When there was only a three-week supply of coal above ground, the steel industry began to operate at half capacity, an embargo was placed on all transportation of freight, and the government ordered a "brown out" to stretch existing coal supplies. A two-week truce was negotiated, the miners returned to work, and just before the truce expired President Truman ordered the mines seized and told Julius A. Krug,

Secretary of the Interior, to negotiate with Lewis. The two came to a quick agreement on the usual 18½ cents increase and a raise in vacation pay. A royalty of 5¢ a ton was to finance a welfare fund that the operators and the union would administer jointly, and the federal government promised to enforce safety regulations.

Meanwhile a strike tied up the country's major railroads; on May 23 trainmen and engineers throughout the nation had left their jobs. To avert a national crisis President Truman begged the strikers to return to their jobs and threatened to operate the railroads (which the government had already seized) with army protection. On May 25 he asked a joint session of Congress to adopt legislation that would give him emergency powers to stop strikes in industries which had been seized by the government. He proposed imprisoning officers of striking unions and drafting into the army all employees who refused to work. A few minutes after President Truman had started to address Congress a note was handed him and he paused to announce:

"Word has just been received that the rail strike has been settled on terms proposed by the President." After the cheering had died down he continued with his speech, and the House of Representatives adopted a bill within a few hours. Labor leaders were stunned and alarmed by the large vote in favor of the proposed law and went to work immediately to arrest the wrath of the antilabor members. Later the Senate removed the draft section from the bill and it was then sidetracked.

In October of that same year, Lewis threatened another strike because he claimed that the government, which was still technically operating the mines, had not lived up to certain agreements. The dispute became involved with legal issues, and on November 18 Federal Judge Alan Goldsborough issued a temporary order restraining union members from leaving their jobs. Lewis refused to obey, and the miners struck. On December 3 the same judge found Lewis guilty of civil and criminal contempt of court, fined him $10,000 and the U.M.W. $3,500,000. The union appealed the decision to the Supreme Court, and Lewis ordered the miners back to work, confident that Goldsborough's decision would be reversed. The following March, the Supreme Court upheld the decision but reduced the fine against the union to $700,000. Eventually Lewis obtained an increase for the miners, but once again his arrogance and defiance of the courts had helped fan the wrath of the anti-unionists. It was questionable how long Congress could withstand pressure from those who feared that unions were becoming too strong, and it was inevitable that legislation curbing labor unions would be passed.

TAFT-HARTLEY

The year 1947 brought a second round of wage increases with a general pattern of fifteen cents an hour. More important, however, were the number of anti-union laws passed by state legislatures. Cooling-off periods, mandatory strike notices, restrictions against picketing, prohibition against closed shops and secondary boycotts, requirements that unions file financial reports, and the legalizing of injunctions in labor disputes composed the bulk of the new legislation.

The numerous, widespread and often crippling strikes, the drives for higher wages, as well as the frightening power which John L. Lewis and some other labor leaders wielded, had aroused many congressmen. In 1946 Congress passed the Lea Act, which curbed the activities of James C. Petrillo, president of the American Federation of Musicians. The Case bill, which was considered during the railroad strike of May, 1946, would have curbed labor unions severely. Although passed by heavy majorities in both the House and Senate, President Truman vetoed it.

The pressure for change continued, however, as many congressmen insisted that the Wagner Act of 1935 made unions too powerful and that the labor laws should be revised. Antilabor forces felt that management's bargaining power should be increased and labor's lessened; that union coercion of employees, breaking of agreements, jurisdictional strikes and boycotts should be prohibited; and that management should again be permitted to "manage" all its employees. To prevent too drastic a change, President Truman prepared a program of his own, but Congress, not to be diverted from its objective, passed the Labor-Management Relations Act, better known as the Taft-Hartley Act. "Shocking—bad for labor, bad for management, bad for the country," was President Truman's description of the bill, but despite his veto Congress passed it a second time on June 23, 1947.

The act represented a compromise between what labor's foes wanted and labor's friends would concede. It allowed employers to sue unions for breach of contract, provided for "cooling-off" periods and presidential use of injunctions in strikes that imperiled national health and safety, prohibited closed shops, forbade union contributions to national elections or primaries and restricted union shops as well as many unfair union practices. The N.L.R.B. was enlarged to five members plus a President-appointed general counsel. Services of the N.L.R.B. were henceforth to be available only to those unions which filed certain financial reports with the Secretary of Labor as well as with their own members. Furthermore,

134

each official of an international or national union had to file an affidavit stating that he was not a Communist.

This provision created a serious problem for the C.I.O., which had enrolled Communists from its earliest days. Communists had controlled locals before World War II in electrical, fur, leather, radio and woodworking industries as well as maritime, municipal and transport workers. Although C.I.O. leaders recognized the danger of including such believers, they knew that most of the workers were loyal Americans and that the Communist-controlled unions would not prove dangerous to the labor movement or threaten the national security. By 1947 Communists still dominated some of the C.I.O. internationals and locals, and an official's failure or refusal to sign an affidavit deprived members of the protections afforded by the law. Walter Reuther lost no time raiding non-Communist locals which were affiliated with internationals that included Communists in their membership. In 1950 the C.I.O. convention expelled seven affiliates that were still Communist-dominated, and the union could then assert it was as free of Reds as its sister organization, the A.F. of L.

"Wildcat" strikes broke out in a number of states as workers protested against the new law; President Truman declared the act was unworkable; William Green denounced the law as "reprehensible and vicious and destructive to the legal and civil rights of workers"; Philip Murray decided to test the ban on political contributions in court; John L. Lewis refused to sign the non-Communist affidavit and withdrew the U.M.W. from the A.F. of L.

As for Senator Robert Taft, one of the law's sponsors, he refuted the President's objections in a radio speech in which he said in part:

"Everyone else in the United States is subject to harassment

135

by lawsuits. Why not unions? . . . We have simply provided that unions are subject to the same general laws as any other corporation or agency or citizen."

Despite its many provisions, the Taft-Hartley Act was not the most restrictive labor act that might have been passed. Although unionists criticized the law generally, they were especially bitter about Section 14(b), which permitted the states to pass right-to-work laws. Undoubtedly Taft-Hartley caused many union men to think about the wisdom of uniting the two largest organizations into a single union in order to present a united front to the common enemy.

REUNION

On November 9, 1952, Philip Murray, who had been president of the C.I.O. for twelve years, died, and within two weeks William Green, president of the A.F. of L. since 1924, died at the age of seventy-two. Walter Reuther succeeded Murray and George Meany, secretary-treasurer of the A.F. of L., became president of that organization.

Young Meany, born in New York City in 1894, attended high school only one year and quit to learn the plumbing trade like his father. He gradually became interested in union activities, was a business agent, secretary of the New York Building Trades Council, state president of the A.F. of L. and since 1939 secretary-treasurer of the national A.F. of L. A big, heavy-set man, resembling the typical old-fashioned cigar-smoking labor leader, he was a reformer, a statesman and sometimes an imaginative leader.

About the time the two labor leaders died, the country elected Dwight Eisenhower, its first Republican president in twenty years. The rank and file wondered what would happen now that Green and Murray were gone and a new President and Congress, both of the "party of big business," were getting ready to run the country. More than ever it seemed that the two major unions should merge into one.

The idea of uniting the A.F. of L. and the C.I.O. had been discussed as early as 1947, by a group of conferees from each union, after the 1946 Republican victory in Congress had alerted all union leaders to the need to halt anti-unionism. Murray, who originally had suggested a merger to William Green, said that a single organization would act "as protection against the ferocious attacks . . . being made upon labor." Misunderstanding resulted after these talks, and although each organization issued statements from time to time, asserting belief in the idea, nothing happened until after Green and Murray died. The officers of the A.F. of L. realized that the Federation's traditional insistence that it represent only craft unions was obsolete, since more than half of its members were in industrial unions. However, the A.F. of L. felt that the most important thing was to achieve unity and that once a merger was accomplished the incidentals could be worked out easily.

A no-raiding agreement, which provided that neither organization would steal members from the other, was signed to become effective July, 1954, and finally on February 9, 1955, the two unions announced that they had completed a pact providing for their merger into one organization, to be known as the A.F. of L.–C.I.O. Under the new arrangement all affiliated national and international unions would maintain their existing status, both craft and industrial unions would be recognized, and leadership would be vested in George Meany as president with Walter Reuther to be second in command.

The merger not only eliminated the competition that existed between the A.F. of L. and the C.I.O. but, more important, made a much stronger organization that could effectively tackle major labor problems and present a better united labor front. It helped strengthen those unionists who were busy fighting corruption and Communists. It eliminated much unnecessary and expensive duplication of administrative expenses and enabled the leaders of the newly created union to pool their energies and abilities.

One criticism leveled at the merged organization was its "bigness," which some people thought would lead to a labor monopoly. When the A.F. of L.–C.I.O.'s newly founded Committee on Political Education (C.O.P.E.) undertook a drive for money to make labor's influence felt in the 1956 presidential election and engaged in an active campaign on behalf of those candidates who were friendly to labor, the union's critics were certain that the combine would become a political threat.

The new A.F. of L.–C.I.O., representing some 15,000,000 workers, was not to become a labor party in politics, George Meany asserted. Instead he immediately turned the union's attention to fighting communism, expelling Red-dominated unions and cleaning out ex-convicts, extortionists and gangsters from the unions. He tried unsuccessfully to break the reputedly corrupt International Longshoremen's Union and bring about other reforms. These honest endeavors at reform were too slight and too late to offset the shocking disclosures of the McClellan Committee, however, and even George Meany found it difficult to believe that so much corruption had permeated some of the unions.

12 ⊂

The Threat of Union Corruption

THE KOHLER STRIKE

JOHN MICHAEL KOHLER EMIGRATED FROM AUSTRIA IN 1873, settled in Sheboygan, Wisconsin (about sixty miles north of Milwaukee), and started a company that at first made farm machinery, then horse watering troughs which could be used also as family bathtubs, and finally a line of bathroom fixtures. Walter Kohler, his son, purchased 2,000 acres of land outside the city in 1912 and laid out a model town complete with recreation areas and community buildings. Employees could borrow money to buy their homes in Kohler Village, a town which resembled an up-to-date residential suburb rather than a drab "company town."

During the depression, when other firms laid off workers, Kohler kept production at capacity and stockpiled bathtubs at a loss of $1,000,000 a year. Kohler looked after its employees,

139

for it was a highly paternalistic firm that had always felt responsible for its workers' welfare. Unfortunately there was a catch to the paternalism. Although the pay was good and living conditions ideal, many employees resented what they called the "feudal system." Workers felt helpless under Kohler supervisors who could downgrade or discipline them at will. They also feared and hated the informer (spy) system which the company justified by saying it needed facts about its employees' behavior.

Early in the 1930's many workers joined the A.F. of L., and later, when the management shortened the workweek to avoid layoffs, there was a strike and trouble. In July, 1934, a riot, complete with tear gas and bullets, ended with two deaths, twenty-eight injured and a broken A.F. of L. union. Under Section 7(a) of the N.R.A. the Kohler management had to bargain with the Kohler Workers Association (a company-sponsored group), but this local had no connection with any outside union and hence no strength. In 1952 the U.A.W., which had extended its activities into many other industries, signed up a majority of the production workers, and two years later there came a showdown as the union demanded, among other things, a twenty cents an hour pay raise, a union shop, union veto power over the company subcontracting any work, promotion according to seniority and a company financed pension plan. Most of these requests had been won by the union elsewhere.

To all the union demands Herbert Kohler, the outraged president, said no, believing that the real issue was whether Kohler or the union was going to run the company. Determined to dig in for what appeared a long fight, Kohler promised that newly hired employees would not be laid off to make way for strikers who later wanted to return. On the other

140

hand, the union asserted that when the strike was settled, every striker would be reinstated.

The U.A.W. called a work stoppage on April 5, 1954, and in violation of federal and state laws, a mass picket line, reinforced with men brought in from outside, many of whom were said to have been hoodlums, even fugitives from the law, quickly surrounded the plant. Once the U.A.W. became determined to win, Walter Reuther threw the force and prestige of the international union behind the strikers. For fifty-four days, while mobs of men picketed illegally, production was halted. The sheriff, who was obviously sympathetic with the strikers, ignored all requests to open the picket line in order to let non-striking employees return to work. Then, under the threat of court action, the size of the picket line was reduced to twenty-five and a pathway cleared to the plant permitting all who wanted to return to work to do so. Some 1,600 reclaimed their jobs, and new employees filled positions once held by those who remained on strike, but it took courage to pass the pickets.

Kohler employees who felt that they had a right to go to work during the U.A.W. strike were painted as enemies of labor. Every day they lived in terror as they heard about or experienced shotgun blasts, beatings, dynamitings, stoning of their homes, picketing in front of their houses by crowds yelling taunts and vulgar words at them, and obscene telephone calls. All told, more than eight hundred instances of violence and vandalism were recorded. The company paid for most of the damage, while the union asserted that it was not responsible for the reign of terror.

When a freighter tied up at Sheboygan with a load of special vitreous clay imported from England, a mob prevented its unloading. The U.A.W. had given the mayor of Sheboygan and the sheriff financial and other support in their political campaigns. As avowed friends of the workingman, these public officials did nothing to protect the Kohler company as it sought to unload the vessel. When the boat moved down the lake to Milwaukee, dock workers and crane operators refused to unload it. Finally at Montreal, with Canadian Mounted Police holding the pickets back, the clay was transferred to freight cars, but the union trainmen refused to cross the U.A.W. picket line at the Kohler plant. Railroad supervisors finally ran the train into the factory.

As the strike entered its third year in 1956, although some $8,000,000 of U.A.W. funds had been spent, production at Kohler had long been normal. Strikers had been supported mostly by Detroit U.A.W. auto workers who had to pay special assessments each month. Now the picket line was reduced to a handful, and most of the strikers either found other jobs or quietly returned to Kohler. Since the strike had been such an obvious failure so far, the union prepared to unleash another weapon, the boycott. After dividing the country into fourteen areas, it formed boycott committees in each and sent out representatives to "unsell" potential Kohler customers from buying their products. "Don't buy Kohler" was their message. The president of the Plumbers Union mailed U.A.W.'s literature to 200,000 members with a personal message asking everyone "to help the Kohler Workers by requesting master plumbers, your employees, your friends, and the purchasing public at large, and other trade union members in your locality, *Not to Purchase Kohler Plumbing Wares and Equipment.*"

Like most boycotts, this was unsuccessful, for the public seldom sympathizes with such tactics. As the strike continued, an N.L.R.B. examiner held hearings from 1955 to 1959. The

McClellan Committee investigated the situation in 1958 and summoned many witnesses, including Herbert Kohler and Walter Reuther, to appear before it. In August of 1960 the N.L.R.B. ruled that Kohler had been guilty of unfair labor practices under the Taft-Hartley Act. The company appealed the decision to the Supreme Court, lost, and then bargained with the union, at last signing a contract on October 7, 1962.

Thus, after eight and a half years, it was difficult to determine who had lost or won. The union, which now claimed membership of only half the workers, had spent $12,000,000 to win fringe benefits estimated to be worth fourteen cents an hour, arbitration of grievances, promotion by seniority and other benefits. It did not gain the wage increase or union shop which were two of the original key issues.

THE McCLELLAN HEARINGS

In Washington D.C. on February 26, 1957, Senator John L. McClellan rapped the gavel and convened the Senate Select Committee on Improper Activities in the Labor or Management Field. He said:

. . . This Select Committee is authorized and directed to conduct an investigation and study of the extent to which criminal or other improper practices or activities are, or have been, engaged in the field of labor-management relations or in groups or organizations of employees or employers to the detriment of the interests of the public, employers or employees, and to determine whether any changes are required in the laws . . . in order to protect such interests against the occurrence of such practices or activities.

One of the committee members was Senator John F. Kennedy; counsel for the committee was his younger brother, Robert.

143

To start its investigation the committee turned its attention toward Oregon, where the *Oregonian,* a Portland newspaper, had published several articles telling of purported ties between officials of the Teamsters' Union, racketeers and politicians. One of the first to testify was Wallace Turner, a reporter for the *Oregonian.* He was called to report about visits he had received from certain union members.

MR. TURNER: I mean the members of the union are scared to death to get out of line.

SENATOR McCLELLAN: They are afraid to tell the truth and to reveal what they know?

MR. TURNER: Yes, sir.

SENATOR McCLELLAN: Their fear is what?

MR. TURNER: That their union cards at least will be taken up and they will be out of employment.

SENATOR McCLELLAN: You are testifying under oath that that is what they have revealed to you in the course of your investigation . . . ?

MR. TURNER: I have been so told by members of that union.

SENATOR MUNDT: . . . by retaliation you mean that they fear that they would lose their means of livelihood?

MR. TURNER: That is one thing that they fear; yes.

SENATOR MUNDT: To be deprived of their jobs, and they could not support their families?

MR. TURNER: Yes, sir.

SENATOR MUNDT: There are other types of retaliation which they fear?

MR. TURNER: Yes, sir; that union has a history in our state of physical violence to people who disagreed with them. . . .

SENATOR MUNDT: You are saying under oath that the men who come to visit you at night are afraid not only of the fact

144

they would lose their jobs and their means of livelihood, but that they might also be subjected to physical violence?

MR. TURNER: Yes, sir.

Another witness called to the stand was James B. Elkins, a gambler who ran a pinball and gambling business in Portland. He admitted meeting with John J. Sweeney, the international organizer for the Teamsters in Portland. Robert F. Kennedy questioned him:

MR. KENNEDY: Did you feel that there was anything peculiar about the head of the Teamsters wanting to meet with you?

MR. ELKINS: Yes. I asked John Sweeney why he was romancing a man in my business, and he said, "Well, no particular reason," only he liked to be friends with people in my type of business, that the Teamsters was a powerful organization, politically, and he understood I had put up quite a bit of money politically now and then and there wasn't any use to wasting it, that we could reach some kind of an agreement on it.

MR. KENNEDY: What kind of an agreement?

MR. ELKINS: Both back the same horse, or the same man.

MR. KENNEDY: Will you recount for the Committee the conversation that you had with Mr. Frank Brewster [president of the Western Conference of Teamsters]?

MR. ELKINS: As near as I can remember it, I came into his room and I first sat down in his little waiting room. Three men came in and looked me over for a couple of minutes and walked out. Then he came in, and I went into his place.

I am looking around, and he said, "You don't have to be so-and-so afraid of me. I don't wire up my place." I said, "I'm not afraid of you wiring it up, Mr. Brewster." He said, "I am going to tell you to start with, I don't like the people

145

you represent." I said, "I don't represent any people, just Jim Elkins."

He said, "Well, I am going to tell you something else. I make mayors and I break mayors, and I make chiefs of police and I break chiefs of police. I have been in jail and I have been out of jail. There is nothing that scares me."

I said, "I don't want to scare you. All I want to be is left alone."

He talked a little more and he got red in the face and he said, "If you bother my two boys, if you embarrass my two boys, you will find yourself wading across Lake Washington with a pair of concrete boots." I believe that was the expression.

I said, "Let us name the boys."

SENATOR McCLELLAN: Who were the two boys?

MR. ELKINS: Clyde Crosby and Bill Langley.

SENATOR McCLELLAN: Crosby was what?

MR. ELKINS: Whatever the position he holds—he is the big man for the Teamsters Union in Portland, and he is in charge of the Portland area, international representative or whatever he is.

SENATOR McCLELLAN: Who was Langley?

MR. ELKINS: He was the district attorney of Multnomah County—Portland, Oregon.

Further testimony showed that the Teamsters tried to monopolize the pinball business in Portland by picketing any store that had machines not bearing union stickers. The object of the picketing was not to organize the employees but to force a payoff to the Teamsters' officials. H. A. Crouch of Portland, Oregon, testified that his Mt. Hood Cafe was picketed by the Teamsters.

MR. KENNEDY: Would you tell the Committee about the picketing—why it was picketed?

146

MR. CROUCH: Yes. I was in the kitchen one morning, working and doing my cooking there, and Mr. Frank Malloy walked in.

MR. KENNEDY: Who is Mr. Frank Malloy?

MR. CROUCH: He belongs to the Teamsters, some way or another. He asked me whose machines I had, and I told him Stan Terry [a Portland pinball operator]. He said, "Well," he says, "Crouch, you better take those machines out, because in a few days you might be picketed." I said, "They can't picket me. I belong to the Culinary Workers."

MR. KENNEDY: What did he say?

MR. CROUCH: He said, "You will find out." So two or three days from then I came to work and he had the pickets in front of me, in front of my place.

MR. KENNEDY: What happened?

MR. CROUCH: I asked Malloy, "You can't do this—what is the big idea?" I told him, "I belong to the restaurant union. Why picket me?" He said, "We are not picketing you. We are picketing Stan Terry's machines. You take Stan Terry's machines out and we will pull the pickets."

SENATOR MUNDT: Did he suggest whose machines you might put in?

MR. CROUCH: A few days after I did take them out one of the Acme men left his card there, and I said, "Are you union?" And he says, "Yes, we are. You will not be bothered." So I took them in.

SENATOR MUNDT: Mr. Crouch, these pickets out in front of your place—were they for the purpose of keeping patrons from coming or keeping deliveries from coming in?

MR. CROUCH: Both. All my customers are railroad-union men, taxicab drivers' union, and they told them not to come in my place. They couldn't cross the picket line.

SENATOR MUNDT: How about the deliveries? Did they cease coming in, too?

MR. CROUCH: Yes. They did. They stopped.

147

Stanley Terry was the biggest distributor of pinball machines in Portland, and subsequently, according to James Elkins, Terry paid $10,000 to Frank Brewster to get into the union and be free of pickets. When questioned later, Terry testified under oath that he had not given Frank Brewster the $10,000.

From Portland, Oregon, the committee's investigation shifted to Teamsters' activities in Scranton, Pennsylvania. Mr. Kennedy asked Paul Bradshaw, former steward for Teamsters Local 229, to tell about the "strong-arm methods" used against the El Rancho Dairy at Scranton.

MR. BRADSHAW: Robert Malloy [business agent for Local 229] called me one morning and he said: "Paul, we are meeting down at the lunchroom and we are having some trouble with a milk concern in Scranton." And so he said, "We're going to go out and give the guy a bad time."

So we met at the lunchroom and it must have been about fifteen or twenty of us altogether, and four or five got in one car and four or five in another car, and we all had instructions to get around to each part of the town.

Some of the boys, including myself, the car I was in, we went up into the country. So we came in contact with one of the drivers and we asked him about organizing and so at the beginning they said they didn't want to organize, and he said he didn't want no part of the union.

So we had two gallon cans filled with kerosene with us which Bob Malloy gave us and with instructions to pour it over the milk, the eggs and the butter in the truck. When we went to do that the man said that he will join, he will join, and that was the end of that, and he did. He signed the slip to join the union.

Those who did not go along were threatened, a truck was overturned, a stink bomb was thrown through a window, a house was blasted. After hearing out the sickening story of

148

violence and terror the committee turned its attention to New York.

After listening to testimony on the activities of Max Block, head of two locals of the Amalgamated Meat Cutters and Butcher Workmen's Union, Locals 342 and 640 in New York City, Senator McClellan said in part:

> The conclusion seems inescapable that Max Block and his family treated these two unions as their own private property, and thousands of dues-paying members were made to suffer accordingly.
>
> They engaged in empire building in the most evil connotation of that term. In this case are the same overtones of denial of democratic process, the seizure and consolidation of power and the concentrated drive for perpetuation in office which the committee has encountered in other cases.

Almost as bad were disclosures revealed when witnesses took the stand and testified on activities of the Laundry Workers, the Hotel and Restaurant Employees, the Operating Engineers of the United Textile Workers and the Bakery and Confectionery Workers. They told of violence, extortion, misuse of union funds and collusion between employees and union leaders.

At length the spotlight swung to Tennessee and here the committee uncovered some of the worst conditions it heard.

THE REIGN OF TERROR

The Newman-Pemberton Corporation, a trucking firm, operated sixty trailers in some ten states. According to J. R. Pemberton of Clinton, Tennessee, secretary-treasurer of the company, the Teamsters' Union wanted to represent only his

149

over-the-road drivers, whom the union said it had signed up. The company asked that an election be held among all drivers but the union refused, whereupon half the employees went on strike and set up picket lines. The company filed for a N.L.R.B. election, but the board answered that first it must investigate certain unfair labor practice charges brought by the teamsters against the company. (These were later dismissed.)

Between June 16 and October 1, 1956, during which time picketing took place:

Mr. Pemberton's phone rang after midnight three of four times a week. Sometimes the caller would just "breathe," other times he would "threaten to bring me in on a slab."

One night during July a company truck was forced off the road near Lexington, Kentucky, by another vehicle. A wrecker dispatched to assist it almost met the same fate. Identification of the attackers was impossible because the rear license plate was not lit.

On the first of August someone fired on a truck near Jellicoe, Tennessee, and two tires were shot. Roy Byrd, manager of the company's Cincinnati terminal, was driving the truck, and although the shooting was reported to the state highway police, "We never heard any more about it."

Three days later seventy-six tires were slashed at the Cincinnati terminal. Costs: $4,000.

On August 9 Roy Byrd was ambushed as he drove his truck and was shot through the shoulder.

On August 21 a Pemberton truck was set on fire. Cost: $850 to fix the truck, $1,050 to repair the burnt garage.

On September 2 Bush Brothers & Company Canneries, where Pemberton kept trucks and equipment, was rocked by dynamite that did damage totaling $25,000. It would have

150

been worse if the other fifty-seven sticks of dynamite had not failed to explode because of a faulty fuse.

Later that month a truck was dynamited in the company's Knoxville lot. Cost for repairs: $1,200.

Two of Bush Brothers' trucks were stopped by Pemberton strikers and told to go back. The strikers had guns to make the orders stick. One of the strikers, Clarence Oakes, was arrested and prosecuted but acquitted.

On October 1—the day the pickets were called off—a truck was shot at, its motor hit and tires ruined. Cost: $6,000.

Between June 16 and October 1, seventeen trucks had been "syruped" (syrup poured in the crankcase), and as a result three motors were ruined, four badly damaged.

By October 1 the N.L.R.B. was ready to call an election, but the union filed a disclaimer of any further interest and as Mr. Pemberton said, they "quit."

The committee questioned Mr. Pemberton about the lack of prosecutions in the dynamiting of Bush Brothers' plant. Mr. Pemberton stated that the county sheriff's office told him that the Tennessee Bureau of Investigators had called off its inquiry into the case.

When called to the witness stand, John T. Reynolds, an investigator for the Tennessee Bureau of Criminal Identification, did not deny that he had told an investigator for the McClellan Committee that he had not tried to get a search warrant to look for a gun used in a Teamsters' shooting because: "We more or less keep out of union trouble," and in this instance it "may have been for political reasons."

Mr. Pemberton's story was merely the leadoff into a series of grim reports of Teamsters' activities. In summing up this part of the hearings, Senator McClellan said:

At the outset of these hearings, I announced that we were

151

going to look into certain aspects of organized goon violence in the state of Tennessee, and in other states in that vicinity. Although fully prepared for some of the more serious aspects of the case, I do not think we were prepared for the shocking pattern of viciousness, lawlessness, and disregard for the laws of the land to which the many witnesses have testified here.

Both the public and Congress were aroused over these revelations of monopoly, racketeering, corruption and crime in certain union circles. During the course of the hearings the committee received nearly 100,000 letters, mostly from union members. Although many were unsigned, for the most part they too told of resentment toward union officials and their methods of dealing with the members. A torrent of mail engulfed Congress, demanding that it do something to curb union abuses.

Anger was especially directed at the thrice-investigated Teamsters' Union and its alleged perpetration of beatings, gangsterism, unsolved murders and stealing from union treasuries. Robert Kennedy stated, "The Teamsters' Union is the most powerful institution in this country aside from the United States government itself. In many major transportation areas the Teamsters control all transportation."

For a time it looked as though legislation might be adopted which would do the labor movement more harm than good, but cooler heads won and Congress passed the Labor-Management Reporting and Disclosure Act of 1959 (better known as the Landrum-Griffin Act). In many ways it tightened the provisions of the Taft-Hartley Act, especially with respect to picketing and setting up boycotts. Three of its most important provisions required all unions to file with the Secretary of Labor complete financial reports annually, to bond officers handling union funds and to stop lending large sums to union

152

members or officers. One person whom the new law did not affect was James R. Hoffa, president of the Teamsters' Union.

JAMES RIDDLE HOFFA

On Valentine's Day, 1913, one of the most powerful men in the United States, James Riddle Hoffa, was born in the little mining town of Brazil, Indiana. His father, a coal driller, died when Jimmy was seven, leaving Mrs. Hoffa to care for herself and four children as best she could. Five years later the family moved to Detroit, and after finishing the seventh grade Jimmy was forced to leave school in order to help support the family.

At the age of seventeen the chunky, young Hoffa was working as a platform loader in a Detroit bakery where he organized the men working with him into a union and obtained a Teamsters' charter. Two years later he sought the presidency of the Detroit Joint Teamsters' Council as well as leadership of the city's three driver locals. Although he received only four of the twenty counsel delegates' votes, he made himself president. "I just walked in and took over," he declared.

Next he founded a state-wide Teamster Conference and advanced to become the state Teamster boss. Now he moved in on businessmen. When twenty-seven, he was indicted by the federal government for conniving with waste-paper collecting companies to establish a monopoly enforced by his union. Included in the indictment was the charge that the waste-paper executive's home had been bombed. Hoffa received a $1,000 fine.

After this the state prosecuted him for violation of a labor law because he had demanded that owners of little grocery stores join the Teamsters and pay dues or have deliveries cut off. He paid a $500 fine and was placed on two years probation.

Those early activities were merely warm-ups for later dealings. By 1952 he had become so powerful that he got the presidency of the Teamsters for Dave Beck and in return became vice president of the union and head of two of its four regional conferences. He was just as influential with those outside the Teamsters. Several other union leaders called on him for help when they needed assistance in conducting strikes or organizing. Those planning to get into labor racketeering who needed union charters also sought out Hoffa. The A.F. of L.–C.I.O., after looking into Hoffa's record, was harsh in condemning his associations with the underworld.

He had also become an important political figure in Michigan, where his lawyer, George Fitzgerald, became the National Democratic Committeeman from Michigan, a position which gave him control over the patronage dispensed by the Truman administration in that state. Hoffa helped elect judges, contributed generously to various political campaigns and even ran his own man for lieutenant governor. When a congressional investigation began to ask Hoffa embarrassing questions, according to Representative Wint Smith of Kansas, "Pressure came from so high that I can't even discuss it," and the hearings ended then and there.

In 1957 the McClellan Committee listed eighty-two charges against Hoffa, accusations that ranged from using terror against members and protecting rackets, to accepting favors from employers and harboring criminals.

A few of the McClellan Committee's conclusions included the following:

Hoffa had sided with convicted extortionists and employers to work against members of his union.

Often, with help of union funds, Hoffa had engaged in many lucrative personal businesses such as obtaining oil leases, running a trucking firm, operating a girls' camp, speculating in land development and backing a prizefighter.

Approximately $2,400,000 of the funds of just one local were "grossly misused for financial assistance to himself, cronies and friends."

Many loans of a questionable nature were made to Hoffa and by Hoffa. One, in the amount of $1,200,000, went to a Minneapolis department store run by a friend of Hoffa's who was struck by another A.F. of L. union.

Officials of Local 619 in Pontiac, Michigan, who were serving prison sentences for extortion, had received $30,000 in legal fees and $85,489 in salaries from the Teamsters.

Paul (The Waiter) Rocca, a notorious member of the Capone gang, received $149,317 of Teamsters' funds with which to purchase his home.

The International Brotherhood of Teamsters, Chauffeurs, Warehousemen and Helpers (which also includes a diversity of occupations such as dairy workers, stenographers, store clerks, brewery workers, gas station attendants, factory workers) is the largest and most powerful union in the United States. The McClellan Committee stated that the Teamsters could "stop the nation's economic pulse" and that "a criminal background was the prerequisite for job placement and advancement within the teamster firmament."

Revelations of the McClellan Committee hearings forced Dave Beck, who was indicted for larceny and income tax evasion, to step down as president of the Teamsters. Immediately Hoffa said he was a candidate for the position, an announcement which prompted the president of the A.F. of L.–C.I.O. to declare that any affiliate which elected corrupt leaders would be expelled. The executive council ordered the bakers, teamsters and textile workers to clean up their unions within thirty days or face expulsion. In clear defiance of the edict, the Teamsters elected James Hoffa president at their Miami convention, and the union was promptly thrown out of the A.F. of L.-C.I.O.

Meanwhile Hoffa was indicted in New York for wire tapping and perjury. In Washington, thirteen New York City teamsters obtained a court injunction forbidding Hoffa from taking the presidency until an investigation was held on the charge that the election was "rigged." Hoffa fought back savagely with every possible legal device—even suing Senator Kennedy and others for libel—and the court finally appointed a board of monitors to supervise the union's conduct of its affairs.

Despite the shocking revelations brought out by numerous court cases and the McClellan hearings, six years after the McClellan Committee had issued its report and the Teamsters had been expelled from the A.F. of L.-C.I.O., James Riddle Hoffa still occupied Dave Beck's former office in the elegant Teamsters' building overlooking the Capitol in Washington, D.C.

13

Pins and Needles

THE SORDID PICTURE OF UNION CORRUPTION PRESENTED IN the last chapter is by no means typical of unionism today. Enlightened union leaders are giving more and more thought to how they may make the union organization and its treasury of greater service to the members. One union that has been rendering unusual service to its members for more than half a century is the International Ladies' Garment Workers' Union (I.L.G.W.U.), which is headquartered in New York City.

A wave of Russian, Romanian and Polish Jews, fleeing from poverty and the czar's pogroms, came to New York in the middle 1890's. Most of them were skilled tailors and settled on the East Side of Manhattan, where they entered the apparel trades. They timed their arrival well, for women in America were just turning to ready-made garments, and a brand new industry was opening up in lower New York. Although it was not long before the beginning of the so-called Progressive Era, everything about the new ladies' garment industry smacked of slavery and the worst possible working conditions.

In the "pig market," the employment agencies that served the garment trade, workers were auctioned off for wages of four to five dollars a week in jobs where they were forced to work as many as twelve hours a day, seven days a week. At that time workers had to pay for their needles and thread and provide their own sewing machines. Peddlers sold the employees bagels (bread rolls twisted into doughnut shapes), which were then hung from hooks so the men and women could munch on them without stopping work. The doors were locked in the morning, and no one was permitted to leave until night unless they became ill. Even the toilets could not be used without special permission of the boss.

A man could establish a business with an investment as small as fifty dollars. All he needed was a tenement room and a few tables for sewing machines. Labor was so plentiful that he could hire people to work for him and make them wait for their wages until he had sold the finished goods. With thousands of these one-room establishments, each operating at a feverish pace, there was endless price cutting, and starvation wages were the rule.

Employers were famous for their chiseling, and the industry was well known for its lack of ethics. Underbidding one's competitors was customary and was accomplished successfully by cutting the workers' wages. With a little luck and limited capital a shrewd man might make a lot of money overnight. From the beginning days of this industry, competition had been ruthless and harsh. Garment manufacturers generally distrusted each other, and for that reason there had never been a single national association of garment makers.

During the late 1800's numerous unions were organized among the oppressed garment workers, but most of the organizations lasted only a short time. In June, 1900, eleven dele-

158

gates from seven union organizations, representing a total of 2,000 members scattered among four cities, met to form the International Ladies' Garment Workers' Union. Little if anything of great importance was accomplished by the new group of workers until 1909, when the union conducted an unsuccessful strike of shirtwaist workers which was dubbed the "uprising of the 20,000." The women picketing in front of their shops were cruelly beaten by employers' hired thugs, and after two months the strike was canceled. It was not in vain, however, for the next year the union prepared more carefully for a walkout—called the "Great Revolt"—that involved some 40,000 cloak makers. This strike brought police brutalities against pickets; but the strikers won their dispute, and in September, 1910, a "Protocol of Peace" was signed. This was the new union's first real victory, and it brought tremendous improvements in working conditions to the long-oppressed garment workers.

No longer would they have to pay for needles, thread and "fines." Home work was abolished and there would be ten holidays. Six days would be the normal workweek, and those who wanted to observe the Jewish Sabbath on Saturday could have the option of working Sundays. The regular workweek would be fifty-four hours with no overtime on Saturdays except after sundown. A Joint Board of Sanitary Control, a Board of Arbitration, and a Committee of Grievances were also established. Pay would hereafter be in cash, and piece workers would receive their money immediately instead of having to wait sometimes indefinitely.

The following year the Triangle Shirtwaist Company fire killed 146 women who were forced to work behind doors that were locked to keep out union organizers. This tragedy brought new laws that further improved working conditions

159

and helped all factory workers. Although the I.L.G.W.U. made little progress in expanding its membership during the next twenty years, it did pioneer a number of "firsts" in the labor movement.

In 1913 the union established the first union health center.

In 1915 the union opened the first vacation center for its members at Pine Hill, New York.

In 1917 the union inaugurated the first educational department for its employees.

In 1919 the union set up the first employer-contributed unemployment compensation plan.

Following the conclusion of World War I some people in this country thought that the Russian Revolution was a sure sign that all workers and peasants would revolt and take over the world. Those Communist sympathizers who belonged to the I.L.G.W.U. believed that the union should help bring about the revolution here. Between 1920 and 1932 the union lost 75 per cent of its members, as the Communists took over. When David Dubinsky was elected president and secretary-treasurer in 1932 the membership had fallen to about 40,000.

THE MAN WHO HATED COMMUNISTS

David Dubinsky was born in Brest Litovsk, Poland, on February 22, 1892. His father soon moved the family to Lodz where he rented rooms in a basement and at night turned the kitchen into a bakery. David, the youngest of six children, started working for his father at thirteen. Two years later he joined the bakers' union, whereupon he was elected secretary because he could read and write. When the bakers struck for higher wages, David led the pickets in front of his father's bake shop. He was also active as a revolutionary Socialist, conspiring against the czarist government in Poland, and at

160

sixteen was arrested because of his political connections and sentenced to a Siberian prison.

It did not take Dubinsky long to find a way of escaping from the prison and making his way back to Lodz, where he hid from the police until his brother Jacob could give him a steamship ticket to New York. He arrived at Ellis Island with his patched suit his only possession. His first job was as a dishwasher earning three dollars a week, a task which left him time to become active in the Socialist party evenings. Seeking to improve himself he became a "cutter" and joined the I.L.G.W.U. Local 10. During the next twenty years he busied himself in union affairs, strongly opposing Communist infiltration and domination of the union.

When Dubinsky became president of the I.L.G.W.U. in 1932 he also was elected to the post of general secretary-treasurer, thereby giving himself strong administrative powers during a crucial period in the life of the organization. In 1959 Louis Stulberg was elected general secretary-treasurer. Dubinsky continued as president, and in 1963 still had to serve until the 1964 convention. A fervent believer in the type of "socialism" represented by the "New Deal," he nevertheless was a profound hater of communism and fought its followers at every opportunity. He drew the I.L.G.W.U. into political action through his founding, with other unions, of the Liberal party in New York State. Dubinsky, often accused by his enemies of being a dictator, is revered by most of the members, who are grateful that under his leadership the union grew steadily and they enjoyed an ever-increasing number of benefits, thanks to his progressive ideas.

Dubinsky was scrupulously honest, and when it came to handling the I.L.G.W.U.'s finances no other union was as careful of its members' funds. Scores of auditors ("my own F.B.I."

161

as Dubinsky referred to them) would roam the country examining the books of local and regional offices, the men arriving for the audits unannounced. In addition an annual financial report, including the staff payroll, issued to every member and widely published, enabled everyone to see exactly how the money was spent.

EDUCATION

Education has been an important activity of the I.L.G.W.U. since 1918, when it pioneered the founding of a workers' university in New York City. Five years later Manhattan had eight such schools, and there were others in Boston and Philadelphia. The schools taught such subjects as American history, literature, economics, music appreciation, trade unionism, physical training and English. Even at Unity Center, the union's $4,000,000 beautiful resort situated on 1,000 acres at Forest Park, Pennsylvania, courses in arts and crafts, music and other subjects are offered.

A union like the I.L.G.W.U. is big business, for it has close to 500,000 members, an annual income of almost $20,000,000 in dues and yearly receipts of some $125,000,000 segregated for health, welfare and retirement benefits. Need for good managers triggered the I.L.G.W.U. Labor College, which holds its classes in New York City. Here union members and other qualified men and women may take the equivalent of a one-year graduate course in union leadership. The free course prepares students for administrative positions within the union and graduates are in great demand.

UNIQUE ACTIVITIES OF A UNIQUE UNION

A successful musical review, *Pins and Needles,* sponsored by the union, ran on Broadway from 1937 to 1941.

162

With These Hands, the first professionally produced union movie, was translated into twelve languages for use overseas by the U. S. State Department.

Millions of dollars of union funds (from special assessments for the purpose) have gone to charitable causes such as the United Jewish Appeal, Boys' Town in Italy and an orphanage in China.

Funds have been sent abroad to help combat communism.

The I.L.G.W.U. instituted the first labor-management engineering department to show garment firms how to operate more efficiently. Trained economists have also been available to give employers advice on business trends.

When one of the I.L.G.W.U. locals had suffered a seven-month strike with no prospects of settling the dispute, the union built a plant nearby which it leased to a competitor who then hired the striking employees.

After twenty-four persons had lost their lives in a fire at the Monarch Undergarment Company in New York City in 1958, the I.L.G.W.U. set up plant inspections. Union members in each factory volunteered to become fire wardens to watch for and report violations of the fire code. Representatives of the New York City Fire Department taught the wardens the rudiments of fire prevention.

In 1959 the union set aside an annual budget of $1,000,000 to promote its union label among customers, thus aiding the fashion industries which employ its members.

As of January 1, 1963, the I.L.G.W.U. had 441,138 members in 432 local unions and contracts covering more than 14,000 plants throughout the United States. Over 80 per cent of its members are women, its unionists representing almost every racial origin found in the country—some twenty-two

163

different nationalities. The union has had only one general strike in twenty-nine years, and its members enjoy not only good wages but also substantial health, welfare, educational and recreational benefits. Little wonder most members are proud of their union, a pioneer in many fields that have only recently become common to all other unions.

14 ⊂

Problems of the Sixties

WHEN PRESIDENT JOHN F. KENNEDY TOOK OFFICE IN 1961 there was bold and optimistic talk about the "new frontier"— a prosperous era that promised economic growth, new horizons and opportunities for all. Labor, which had helped elect the Democratic President and Congress, expected that it too would share in the fruits of the victory.

By 1963 the optimistic picture had changed somewhat. The previous spring's prices on the stock market had dropped sharply, and the economy had remained sluggish as business failed to boom. Unemployment was rising because the population explosion was expanding the labor force faster than industry could create new jobs, and more than a million young people under twenty-five were out of work. The Administration was sympathetic to labor, although it had spoken out mildly against the crippling strikes of the longshoremen and the New York printers during January of 1963. Many observers felt that if the threatened nation-wide railroad strike materialized, Congress would speedily adopt legislation to curb the power of labor unions.

Labor was responsible for four problems of the sixties which the nation faced: union monopoly, the union shop, featherbedding—the practice of limiting work—and the thirty-five hour workweek. On the other hand, many working people were victims of two situations which were still unsolved: "equal pay for equal work" and discrimination in hiring. Finally, there was the number one problem that faced the entire labor force and threatened the country's economic well-being: automation.

UNION MONOPOLY

Every port on the East and Gulf coasts of the United States was shut down from December 23, 1962, to January 25, 1963, by the International Longshoremen's Association when it refused to eliminate featherbedding and accept reduced work crews. Shippers' operations were paralyzed. A hundred thousand people were thrown out of work, and the public was forced to do without services which the dock workers and shippers normally provided. The United States government was embarrassed in its Alliance for Progress program in South American countries where the strike brought great hardship to some nations. The cost to the country was almost a billion dollars.

Referring to this strike James Hoffa said:

There can be no individual strikes of transportation in an individual city without affecting widespread areas. The longshoremen's strike is a perfect example. At no time during this controversy of the longshoremen has one single voice been raised that the longshoremen were right. And the government would not have intervened in this strike if one pier had been

166

tied up. Nobody would have raised a voice in behalf of the workers had they been confined to one particular area, one given dock; only when they had the strike activity over the entire shipping industry was there a successful bringing to a termination of that strike for the benefit of the workers. We feel the same thing applies to transportation and trucks.

While the dock workers were on strike and for more than two months thereafter, striking printers in New York City forced the largest newspapers to cease publication, deprived the public of its daily printed news sources, denied business important media in which to advertise, and caused great economic hardship to all those who handled newspapers or supplied materials and services to the publishers.

Crippling strikes like these which ignored the public interest were hardly news, for the nation had suffered through many in recent years. During 1962 three strikes in the transportation industry had been particularly costly. Flight engineers shut down Eastern Air Lines for most of the summer, then the Order of Railroad Telegraphers halted all operations of the Chicago and North Western Railway and finally the dock workers walked off their jobs.

Neither ethics nor the law requires that industry-wide national unions be responsible to anyone except their members. No antitrust law prohibits them from bargaining with a single industry on wages or working conditions that will apply throughout the nation. No statute curbs the labor leader who in effect says that if the employers refuse to grant the wage increase, fringe benefits, reduced working hours, featherbedding or whatever his demand happens to be, he will call a strike which may threaten the economic well-being of many companies and their employees, harm a large metropolitan area or even damage the entire nation.

167

Few people favor curbing or eliminating the right of an employee to strike, because that would mean compulsory labor. The Norris–La Guardia Act of 1932 guaranteed the right to strike, for it contained language that virtually stopped court injunctions in labor disputes. Thirty years later, thanks to additional federal legislation and court decisions, actions that would be considered antitrust violations by business groups were not deemed illegal when performed by unions, so long as the unions acted in their self-interest and did not combine with non-union groups.

In 1961 Senator John McClellan introduced a bill that would have curbed union power, but it failed to become law. In January, 1963, he and eight associates introduced two new measures to apply antitrust laws to transportation unions and to prohibit strikes or work stoppages at missile sites and other defense facilities.

Speaking before the United States Chamber of Commerce in January, 1963, Senator McClellan said:

It is my view that there are times—possibly many times—when the public interest and the general welfare transcend in importance, the interest and welfare of the two disputing parties, labor and management. And yet today, in such circumstances, we have but one remedy provided by law and that is the inadequate remedy of the Taft-Hartley eighty-day injunction.

It is not the right to strike an employer that I am trying to restrain; rather, I am trying to restrain strikes which in effect are directed against the public. That, in effect, is where these strikes which spread all over the country are directed. Such strikes are in reality directed against the public interest and against the government to a greater extent than they are against management or business.

168

Representative Dave Martin also introduced a bill in 1963 that would "prevent the application or exercise of monopoly power by employers and labor organizations in employing or representing labor. . . ." In a statement to the House he explained that his legislation

> . . . still allows strikes. It restores union power to the local labor unions and takes it out of the hands of the international unions. I repeat, this bill does not interfere with any legitimate labor objectives but only eliminates those activities not in the public interest. Industry-wide bargaining would be eliminated. It would be illegal for two unions to confer with one another in regard to the settlement of a wage dispute.

Union leaders feared that placing unions under antitrust laws would greatly weaken their ability to represent the membership. However, there appeared to be a limit to how far public opinion would tolerate crippling and costly strikes. There was danger that the act of an irresponsible leader might bring harsh reprisals instead of reasonable restraints on the entire labor movement. There was good reason to fear the legislators' wrath, for already many of the states had taken matters into their own hands and adopted laws which outlawed the union shop.

RIGHT-TO-WORK

When the workers at California missile plants went to vote on the union shop in November, 1962, both the government and the unions were confident that the proposal would be overwhelmingly approved. Even President Kennedy criticized the company's opposition as old-fashioned.

"Most major industrial companies or industries accepted the union shop many years ago," he said. "The union shop is part of collective bargaining." Should a strike develop over this issue the President warned that "the responsibility would be very clear, I think, to the American people."

Nevertheless, the companies agreed to permit a vote and employees of General Dynamics, North American Aviation and Ryan Aeronautical went to the polls and to the surprise of everyone—rejected the union shop!

A few weeks later at nearby Douglas Aircraft Company, 1,500 employees faced dismissal for refusing to pay union fees. Under the provisions of a contract signed with the U.A.W. and the International Association of Machinists, which represented workers at four plants, Douglas had to fire all non-union employees who refused to pay "fees" to the union instead of dues. There was some hope that the discharged workers might regain their jobs, because about that same time the Supreme Court agreed to review two lower court decisions which had ruled that agency shops (arrangements where non-union employees must pay "fees") were illegal.

A survey conducted in 1959 by the United States Department of Labor revealed that union shop provisions were incorporated into 71 per cent of the major collective bargaining contracts then in effect, which covered 74 per cent of the workers. Where there is a union shop agreement, employees must join within a certain time, usually sixty to ninety days, or lose their jobs.

A union that represents a majority of a company's employees understandably feels it is not fair for non-members to share all of the wage increases and other benefits which it has spent money to win. As a partial solution to the problem, the "agency shop" was devised to obtain financial aid from non-union members, but obviously any union would rather win a closed shop where it could represent every employee.

Those who object to compulsory unionism believe that it is contrary to our American way of life to force a man to join any kind of organization and contribute to its financial support. The closed shop, or compulsory unionism, they say, helps to create union monopoly.

To combat the union shop, twenty states had enacted right-to-work laws by 1963. According to a study based on United States Department of Labor statistics, from 1953 to 1960 states with right-to-work laws outstripped the non–right-to-work states in the rate of industrial expansion, creation of new jobs and the rate of improvement in hourly wages. Admittedly there is no proof that the right-to-work laws created these favorable conditions, and a survey conducted by *Fortune* revealed that right-to-work laws have little effect on labor union membership.

Both the Wagner Act and the Taft-Hartley Act have forbidden discrimination "in regard to hire or tenure of employment or any term or condition of employment to encourage or discourage membership in any labor organization." Until these laws are amended or repealed, employers are not obligated to compel employees to join a union or lose their jobs. When collective bargaining has resulted in a contract that requires compulsory unionism, both labor and management have disregarded the rights of the individual worker.

Another problem causing serious difficulties during the sixties was that of featherbedding—the practice of limiting work or output in order to provide more jobs and prevent unemployment.

FEATHERBEDDING

The train slowed as it crossed the New York–Pennsylvania border near Binghamton, New York, and a man jumped off. He

171

made his way to a warm trailer where he ate his lunch, talked and napped. Three hours later he hopped on board another train traveling in the opposite direction. For doing little more than looking out of the window during his 100-mile round trip that day the man received more than twenty dollars. He was one of almost 10,000 workers who cost the railroads $74,000,000 annually in unnecessary pay because of "full crew" laws still on the statutes of fifteen states.

Featherbedding in national railroad contracts was estimated in 1963 to cost our nation's carriers $592,000,000 every year. That same year the Supreme Court ruled that railroads might modernize their work rules and eliminate many unnecessary jobs, but this decision did not affect state laws, either those still on the books or those to be adopted. When the Supreme Court decision was handed down, unions in Oregon were pressing for four brakemen on freights of more than one hundred cars, while at the same time the railroads were trying to reduce the number of brakemen from three to two on trains of forty cars.

The practice of featherbedding is not limited to the railroads. A New York court awarded ten ship engineers who had not lost their jobs severance pay equal to a year's salary. The award, which would cost the Grace Line, Inc., an estimated $200,000, was based on a labor contract that provided whenever the company transferred a vessel to foreign registry, the engineers assigned to that ship would receive a year's severance. All of the engineers were placed on other Grace Line ships, and none had lost any pay.

In New York City lumber used in new building construction cannot be hoisted from the ground but must be passed up from floor to floor by hand. In Hollywood a union plumber must be paid a full day's wage if he is required to turn off a faucet

172

once during a day of movie making. In some areas, when trailer trucks are left sitting in a terminal overnight, work rules require that a man stay and "baby-sit" with it, a practice that costs one medium-size company over $10,000 a year.

Featherbedding, of which these are but a few examples, has sprung up whenever the protective instinct of a union has seen jobs threatened by employers' cost-cutting practices or techno-logical advances. A few featherbedding practices have arisen from greed or a union's desire to extend its power, but this has not generally been the case. The solution to the problem is not easy because unions understandably will not submit readily to job reduction that will bring loss of membership and bargaining power. Employers, on the other hand, face hostile union resistance to any cost-cutting through job reduc-tion and will probably be saddled with burdensome expenses as they assume long-term responsibilities for workers who are laid off. Nevertheless, featherbedding appeared to be on its way out after the Supreme Court ruling that railroads had the right to reduce manpower in order to operate more efficiently. Union leaders then turned to another device they hoped would protect existing jobs and create need for additional workers. This could be accomplished by shortening employees' work-ing hours, thus making more job opportunities.

WAGE RISE IN DISGUISE

"If we shorten the workweek to thirty-five hours we will partly solve the unemployment problem," labor leaders said in 1963. What they did not say was that they wanted the work-week shortened to thirty-five hours but with no reduction in pay. Thus, if a company had to give the same wages for fewer hours of work, the cost of its product or service would be in-

173

creased, thereby probably causing sales to drop and layoffs to become necessary.

It was reported that the A.F. of L.–C.I.O. admitted that the thirty-five hour workweek was not a cure-all but a tool to help combat unemployment. The real intent of the drive for the thirty-five hour week was to goad the Administration into adopting some type of economic program that would create jobs. Thus the thirty-five hour week was a means of dealing with unemployment, though some of labor's experts believed that a shorter workweek would increase, not decrease, unemployment.

"We must work, not less but more," Arthur Goldberg said as he resigned his post of Secretary of Labor in 1962. "Neither labor nor management will find the answer to the problems of unemployment and unused capacity in a division of available work or production."

Business offered an alternate solution to the thirty-five hour workweek as a means of solving unemployment. It claimed that the way to put people to work was to expand the economy and encourage industry to invest more money in plants and equipment in order to produce more jobs.

The problems just discussed were not the only labor-management differences that required solution. Many companies paid women lower salaries than men for comparable work and discriminated against Negroes and minority groups when hiring new employees.

"EQUAL PAY FOR EQUAL WORK"

Who can find fault with such a slogan? Unfortunately it is only a slogan; if it were a fact "The Equal Pay Bill of 1962" would not have been introduced into the House of Representatives with the hope of ensuring that women receive the same amount of pay as men when both are performing the same kind of work.

According to Mrs. Esther Peterson, Assistant Secretary of Labor:

". . . a retailer seeking an accounting clerk offered $42 for a woman employee and $45 for a man worker. A distillery with a clerk-typist job to be filled offered $1.87 an hour for a woman employee and $2.19 for a man worker. An electrical manufacturer with a job opening for an assembler offered $1.40 an hour for a woman worker and $1.55 an hour for a man employee."

To the Select Subcommittee on Labor she reported: "While . . . differences in average income result from a variety of factors, persistent differences in earnings of men and women in comparable occupation classifications suggest the need for equal pay legislation as a first step toward more equitable treatment of women."

Those who oppose such a law point out that rates of pay can be misleading because the more frequent absenteeism and higher turnover among women add to the employer's costs and often make it necessary for him to offer less pay to women. Furthermore, most young women entering the labor force look forward to marriage and raising a family, not undertaking a business career. Because some women switch positions frequently, employers incur costly training expenses. Many pension plans permit women to retire earlier than men; employers pay higher insurance premiums on women than men; and many state laws provide shorter hours of work and better working conditions for women than men.

Twenty-two states had in 1963 equal pay laws which varied in coverage and effectiveness. Businessmen argued that it is better to let each state solve its own problem rather than resort

175

to federal legislation. They maintained that education, competition and collective bargaining would gradually eliminate discrimination on the basis of sex and that trying to achieve the goal through federal regulation would create more problems than it would solve.

The Administration, women's organizations and the A.F. of L.–C.I.O. advocated federal legislation because they did not believe all the states would pass such laws or that moral persuasion, competition or collective bargaining would ensure equal pay. There was no guarantee that federal legislation, adopted in 1963, would end such inequalities, however, because many employers broke the law in states that forbade discrimination in hiring.

DISCRIMINATION IN HIRING

"We'll take high type number twos but prefer number ones." "Send us fours."

A search of some employment agencies in northern New Jersey revealed these codes used by certain companies in requesting applicants. White people were ones, Negroes twos and fours. All such practices were violations of the state's antidiscrimination law, which forbids any reference to color or race when hiring.

Discrimination in hiring has always been a problem for Negroes and other minority races. Many states have enacted antidiscrimination laws, but they have proven difficult to enforce. In 1962 one hundred of the country's largest unions signed agreements with the President's Committee on Equal Opportunities to end discrimination within their ranks. Unions stated that signing the agreements was proof of their sincerity to honor their long-standing promise to improve Negro job opportunities.

Anxious to see results instead of continued promises, Roy Wilkins, Executive Secretary of the National Association for the Advancement of Colored People (N.A.A.C.P.), filed charges of discrimination with the N.L.R.B. in 1962. The A.F. of L.–C.I.O. charged that these were "baseless" and liable to strain relations between the N.A.A.C.P. and the A.F. of L.–C.I.O. President George Meany contended that there undoubtedly was discrimination at the local level of unions but that machinery was available to cope with the problem and that it would be better to settle matters that way rather than to file complaints with the N.L.R.B.

Another attack on the problem was begun in March, 1960, when Negro ministers in Philadelphia requested members of their congregations not to patronize certain stores or companies that either did not hire Negroes or denied Negroes advancement and job equality. Bakeries, dairies, soft drink bottlers, gasoline stations, chain stores, were among the twenty-odd companies that felt the effect of the boycott during its first three years. Most of the companies suffered a drop in business and eventually gave in to the Negro demand. The movement of boycotting one company at a time quickly spread to other cities and has differed from the approach used in some southern cities, where Negroes boycotted an entire business district.

This form of protest is safer than sit-ins and public demonstrations, which often lead to violence. Usually economic pressure can get results. The success of the local boycotts moved the Reverend Martin Luther King of Atlanta to work for national boycotts of companies that discriminate against Negroes in hiring. Although there may be some question as to whether or not boycotts of this type are fair, they are usually effective and, in the opinion of those who employ them, fully justified.

Union monopoly is of concern to many Americans. Discrimination can spell tragedy to the man whose color or race bars him from a decent job. The right to work without having to join a union is vital to men who believe the union shop is a denial of their freedom. These are high on the list of serious labor problems that confront our country today, but probably none are as complex or as important as one which threatens the security of millions of jobholders—the new technology or, as it is better known, "automation."

AUTOMATION AND THE LABOR FORCE

R. H. Macy Co., New York's giant department store, introduced its first electronic salesgirl recently. She (the machine) could sell thirty-six different items in ten different sizes and styles, accept coins, one and five dollar bills and return the correct change as well as reject counterfeit currency.

Automatic elevators have eliminated thousands of operators throughout the country. In the chemical industry, production jobs fell 3 per cent during a five-year period while automatic equipment helped output rise 27 per cent. In 1960 the United States Census Bureau needed only fifty statisticians in California to do the tabulations that required 4,100 men and women in 1950. During a ten-year period the Bell System's volume of calls rose 50 per cent with only a 10 per cent increase in personnel.

We have developed amazing machines and processes that automatically perform tasks which often replace and improve upon human capabilities. In addition there are computers which can do either simple or complex decision-making tasks. Once these machines have been given data, they are capable of solving problems, remembering and searching for information, and even making judgments.

178

A broad new term, *cybernation,* has crept into our language. This refers to linking a computer (which interprets complex data and then gives instructions electronically) to a machine which then automatically produces materials or performs certain tasks as directed by the computer. An example of cybernation is the computer in an automobile plant which issues electronic instructions to a machine that feeds unfinished parts of a steering assembly into a trimming press and then controls the press as it completes the fabrication of the parts.

Many benefits may be reaped from automation and cybernation. Machines can perform numerous menial and dull tasks; they can cut production costs and make available certain products in greater quantities at cheaper prices; they can help management make better decisions; they can help increase our national productivity so that we can keep pace with the population growth; and they may eventually help bring us more leisure time.

On the other hand, they have already created a serious unemployment problem which will become greater as automation spreads. Most of the more than 300,000 unemployed in Illinois in 1962 were victims of automation. In California the change in production from manned military aircraft to guided missiles eliminated 200,000 production jobs. It has been estimated that the trend toward automation is displacing approximately 1,800,000 workers each year. This is only part of the unemployment picture, however.

During the 1960's we shall need to create 13,500,000 new jobs just to keep up with the expected growth in the labor force. Stated another way, we shall require an average of 25,000 new jobs every week in addition to those needed to put the unemployed to work and replace jobs eliminated by automation.

Automation will continue to eliminate work opportunities in the very fields where unskilled young people were once able to find their first jobs. By 1965 the annual rate of new job seekers will climb from 2,000,000 to 2,500,000 and by 1970 to 3,000,000. Severe unemployment will face school dropouts; Negroes and other minority groups will continue to face the additional handicap of discrimination; and two-thirds of the rural young people will move to urban areas during the 1960's and seek jobs there. The young person who does not prepare himself or herself properly for a career is going to find it increasingly difficult to earn an adequate living.

Automation, as noted, has reduced employment, and while technology continues to spread, it will dislodge more and more workers from their jobs. This will hurt many unions and especially the old C.I.O. industrial type organizations like the soft coal miners whose union ranks have suffered a considerable drop during recent years. Membership in Walter Reuther's U.A.W. had fallen to 1,000,000 by 1963, a loss of some 250,000 members since the A.F. of L.–C.I.O. merger in 1955. We have already observed the gathering storm clouds in the aircraft missile industry, where workers rejected the union shop at three major companies in 1962.

Trade unions are here to stay despite automation, certain antilabor sentiment, business lobbying and congressional action to curb union monopoly. The history of the labor movement is evidence that unions have filled a vital place in our society and that without them workingmen would again be exploited and the many rights and benefits they have won over the last hundred years would be endangered.

March 1, 1963, was a memorable date for labor because it marked the start of a revolutionary pact agreed to by the Kaiser Steel Corporation and the United Steel Workers. This

180

agreement attempted to solve some of the economic and human problems that face an industrial company and quite possibly was destined to become the forerunner of a "new look" for labor.

Basically the contract was a productivity-sharing plan which gave workers a third share of all cost savings, whether these were achieved through adopting new processes, better materials or improved efficiency of the workers. In addition, personnel were guaranteed against loss of employment or income due to automation and were promised they would receive any wage increase or other economic improvement thereafter negotiated by basic steel producers.

It was the hope of labor and management that the plan would enable the company to make a better and less costly product which would lead to an increased demand for Kaiser steel and thereby create more jobs. They felt that this was a more constructive approach to meeting the problem of automation than reducing the workweek to thirty-five hours. If labor and industry adopted this idea elsewhere perhaps it would help solve the problem of growing unemployment.

WHAT OF THE FUTURE?

Traditionally, labor unions have spent most of their energies organizing, fighting for higher wages and bargaining for shorter hours. According to Chairman Frank W. McCulloch of the N.L.R.B., during the 1960's labor unions will shift their emphasis from wages to other areas and concentrate their efforts on protecting their members from the adverse effects of changing business techniques, public opinion and foreign competition. They will also be greatly concerned with job security.

There were hopeful signs that relations between manage-

181

ment and labor might show improvement. A few companies like Alan Wood Steel held continuing talks with the union to avoid disputes that might lead to a strike. The Human Relations Committee established by the steelworkers and the steel industry endeavored to solve work rules problems. At the request of the U.A.W., Ford and General Motors agreed in March, 1963, to meet individually with union representatives to consider setting up "joint study" committees. According to Walter Reuther such groups would "explore the issues which will confront us when bargaining starts" and thereby help speed up a settlement and minimize the chance of a strike. Perhaps Reuther realized that collective bargaining was on trial for its survival after a series of serious strikes in 1962 and early 1963, when many ended with federal intervention after collective bargaining had failed.

Secretary of Labor Willard Wirtz warned that in critical industries collective bargaining faced its "last clear chance" to work out differences between management and labor. William E. Simkin, director of the Federal Mediation and Conciliation Service stated: "There is a real danger that because of a few highly publicized strikes people will get discouraged and demand drastic changes. One extreme result could be government imposition of settlements on a widespread basis."

Since 1842 when workingmen won the right to band together into unions, and as groups talk and negotiate with employers, collective bargaining has been the American way of settling disputes between management and its organized employees. There is no satisfactory substitute for this democratic process that preserves our American ideal of individual freedom in a competitive economy. At times the labor movement has been turbulent, often bloody, as employers and workmen opposed each other and fought for what each felt was right;

nevertheless collective bargaining has survived and stood the test of time.

If employers had always been considerate of their employees there might never have been any need for workers to band together and form unions. Although injustices like bad working conditions, subsistence wages, long hours and sudden lay-offs were sometimes caused by greed, more often they were brought about by management's need to earn a profit in order to remain in business. Today enlightened management treats its employees fairly and in some cases gives them a share in the profits of the enterprise. There are many large organizations which employ, for the most part, white collar employees who do not belong to any union. Without union contracts to protect them these workers nevertheless receive good wages and generous fringe benfits such as pension plans, bonuses, paid insurance, vacations that increase with seniority, recreational facilities and numerous paid holidays, thus proving that all employees do not have to belong to unions in order to receive fair treatment.

In the early sixties there were many hopeful signs that organized labor would have less need to resort to strikes in order to gain its just demands and that labor and management would learn to settle their differences amicably and without the help of the federal government. Labor and management can show the world that our free enterprise system will continue to bring security and happiness to nearly two hundred million Americans as they work together toward the common goal of a more prosperous America.

Suggested Reading

Any of the following books you cannot find in your public or school library should be obtainable through an interlibrary loan which your librarian can arrange. For up-to-date material on labor leaders see recent volumes of the *Biographical Index* and for current information on labor problems, consult the *Readers' Guide to Periodical Literature*.

Automation and Cybernation

Calder, Nagel, *Robots*. New York, Roy Publishers, 1958.
Diebold, John, *Automation, the Advent of the Automatic Factory*. New York, Van Nostrand, 1952.
Michael, Donald N., *Cybernation: The Silent Conquest*. Santa Barbara, California, The Fund for the Republic, Inc., 1962.

Current Labor Problems

Daniels, Walter M. (Editor), *The American Labor Movement*. New York, H. W. Wilson Company, 1958.

The Depression

Shannan, David A. (Editor), *The Great Depression*. Englewood, New Jersey, Prentice-Hall, Inc., 1960.

Werstein, Irving, *A Nation Fights Back—The Depression and Its Aftermath*. New York, Julian Messner, Inc., 1962.

The Kohler Strike

Petro, Sylvester, *The Kohler Strike*. New York, Henry Regnery Company, 1961.

Labor History

Commons, John R. and others, *History of Labor in the United States* (four volumes). New York, The Macmillan Company.

Dulles, Foster R., *Labor in America*. New York, Thomas Y. Crowell Company, 1960.

Rayback, Joseph G., *A History of American Labor*. New York, The Macmillan Company, 1961.

Roe, Wellington, *Juggernaut—American Labor in Action*. New York, J. B. Lippincott Company, 1948.

Velie, Lester, *Labor U.S.A.* New York, Harper & Brothers, 1958.

Labor in Colonial America

Morris, Richard B., *Government and Labor in Early America*. New York, Columbia University Press, 1946.

Phillips, U. B., *Life and Labor in the Old South*. Boston, Little, Brown and Company, 1930.

Labor in the Early Nineteenth Century

Riegel, Robert E., *Young America, 1830-1840*. Norman, Oklahoma, University of Oklahoma Press, 1949.

Labor Leaders

Ginger, Ray, *Eugene V. Debs*. New York, Collier Books.

Danish, Max D., *The World of David Dubinsky*. New York, World Publishing Company.

Foster, William Z., *Pages from a Worker's Life*. New York, International Publishers, 1961.

Taft, P. and Sessions, J. A. (Editors), *Seventy Years of Life and Labor, an Autobiography of Samuel Gompers.* New York, E. P. Dutton & Company, 1957.

Fisher, Dorothy F., *American Portraits* (William Green). New York, Henry Holt, 1946, pages 110-112.

Madison, Charles A., *American Labor Leaders.* New York, Frederick Unger Publishing Company, 1962, pages 108-135.

Collier's Encyclopedia 1958 Yearbook (James Hoffa). P. F. Collier & Son Corporation, 1959, pages 699-700.

Daniels, Walter M., *The American Labor Movement.* New York, H. W. Wilson Company, 1958, pages 192-197.

Alinsky, Saul, *John L. Lewis, an Unauthorized Biography.* New York, G. P. Putnam's Sons, 1949.

Wechsler, James A., *Labor Baron, a Portrait of John L. Lewis.* New York, William Morrow and Company, 1944.

Current Biography, 1954 (George Meany). New York, H. W. Wilson Company, 1955, pages 450-452.

Robinson, Donald B., *100 Most Important People.* New York, Pocket Books, 1953.

Madison, Charles A., *American Labor Leaders* (John Mitchell). New York, Frederick Ungar Publishing Company, 1962, pages 157-172.

Current Biography, 1949 (Philip Murray). New York, H. W. Wilson Company, 1950, pages 444-447.

Madison, Charles A., *American Labor Leaders.* New York, Frederick Ungar Publishing Company, 1962, pages 295-334.

Christman, Henry M. (Editor), *Walter P. Reuther, Selected Papers.* New York, The Macmillan Company, 1961.

Howe, Irving and Widick, B. J., *The UAW and Walter Reuther.* New York, Random House, 1949.

Labor on the Assembly Line

Walker, C. R. and Guest, R. H., *The Man on the Assembly Line.* Cambridge, Massachusetts, Harvard University Press, 1952.

Labor Organization

Hardman, J. B. S. and Neufeld, M. F., *The House of Labor, Internal Operations of American Unions.* New York, Prentice-Hall, Inc., 1951.

Sayles, L. R. and Strauss, George, *The Local Union: Its Place in the Industrial Plant.* New York, Harper & Brothers, 1953.

Labor Racketeers

Seidman, Harold, *Labor Czars, a History of Labor Racketeering.* New York, Liveright Publishing Corporation.
(See also McClellan Hearings below)

McClellan Hearings

Kennedy, Robert, *The Enemy Within.* New York, Harper & Brothers, 1960.

Petro, Sylvester, *Power Unlimited, the Corruption of Union Leadership* (a report on the McClellan Committee hearings). New York, The Ronald Press Company, 1959.

Mining Problems

Angle, Paul M., *Bloody Williamson, a Chapter on American Lawlessness.* New York, Alfred Knopf, 1952. (Story of the Herrin Massacre of 1922.)

Gilfillan, Lauren, *I Went to Pitt College.* New York, Viking Press, 1934. (Vivid story of how miners lived during the depression.)

Lord, Walter, *The Good Years.* New York, Harper & Brothers, 1960, also in Bantam paperback edition, pages 76-80. (John Mitchell and the miners' strike of 1902.)

Strikes After World War II

Goldman, Eric F., *The Crucial Decade, America 1945-1955.* New York, Alfred A. Knopf, 1956.

Index

188

189

190

Union corruption, 139-156
Union monopoly, 166-169
Union shop, 169-171
United Automobile Workers, 92-99, 106, 121, 123-129, 140-143, 170, 182
United Brotherhood of Carpenters and Joiners of America, 84
United Mine Workers of America, 41-44, 67-69, 77, 85, 88, 113-115, 131-133
United States Steel Corporation, 66, 89, 90
United States Supreme Court, 58, 81, 82, 90, 99, 109-110, 133, 143, 170, 173
United Steelworkers of America, 92, 180-181
United Textile Workers, 56, 79-80, 118

Virginia Company, 8-9

Wagner Act, 82-83, 90, 99, 109-110, 134, 171
War Labor Board, 111-113, 115, 116, 119
Western Federation of Miners, 52-54
Western Labor Union, 53-54
Whitney, Eli, 31
Wierton case, 81-82
Wisconsin Light and Power Company, 108
Women's Committee of Philadelphia, 56
Working conditions, 1820-1840, 21-24; in coal fields, 40-41; for women and children, 58-59; during 1920's, 70-71; in garment industry, 157-158
Working Man's Advocate, 27
Workingmen's Party, 25-28
Wright, Frances (Fanny), 27-28
World War II, 111-112, 120

"Yellow dog" contracts, 70, 72, 110

About the Author

ADRIAN A. PARADIS was born in Brooklyn, New York, educated in public and private schools and graduated from Dartmouth College. He sold encyclopedias, worked for a literary agent, was a private secretary and managed his own hotel. He returned to college, Columbia University's School of Library Service, and at the same time worked as a law librarian. Upon graduation in the spring of 1942, he joined American Airlines to start a company economic library. Subsequently he served as office manager, financial analyst and since 1947 as Assistant Secretary in charge of corporate work. Writing is a hobby with Mr. Paradis, and since his first book appeared in 1950 he has authored thirteen other books, numerous articles and syndicated columns.